Pittsburgh Series in Bibliography

JAMES GOULD COZZENS

James Gould Cozzens

A DESCRIPTIVE BIBLIOGRAPHY

Matthew J. Bruccoli

UNIVERSITY OF
PITTSBURGH PRESS
1981

In Memory of
Vern Sternberg

Downheartedness was no man's part. A man must stand up and do the best he can with what there is. If the thing he labored to uncover now seemed in danger of stultifying him, could a rational being find nothing to do? If mind failed you, seeing no pattern; and heart failed you, seeing no point, the stout, stubborn will must be up and doing. A pattern should be found; a point should be imposed.

Published by the University of Pittsburgh Press, Pittsburgh, Pa. 15260
Copyright © 1981, University of Pittsburgh Press
All rights reserved
Feffer and Simons, Inc., London
Manufactured in the United States of America

Library of Congress Cataloging in Publication Data

Bruccoli, Matthew Joseph, 1931–
    James Gould Cozzens: a descriptive bibliography.

    (Pittsburgh series in bibliography)
    Includes index.
    1. Cozzens, James Gould, 1903–   —Bibliography.
I. Series.
Z8196.9.B78   [PS3505.'99]   016.813'52   80-24689
ISBN 0-8229-3435-3

Contents

Acknowledgments

ALL good bibliographies are collaborations. I am indebted to the following: W. R. Anderson, Huntington College; Australian National University Library; Carol Brandt, Brandt & Brandt; Fannie Collins; Joseph Covino, Great Neck Public Library; Thayer Cumings; Col. Joseph M. Dougherty; J. A. Edwards, University of Reading Library; Lori Finger, Cooper Library, University of South Carolina; Suzanne Gleaves; Maj. James A. Grimshaw, Jr., Air Force Academy; Marilla B. Guptil, National Archives and Records Service; A. M. Heath Agency; Cara Irvin, Book-of-the-Month Club; Samuel W. John, Kent School; William Jovanovich, Harcourt Brace Jovanovich; Joan Judge, Harcourt Brace Jovanovich; Col. Frederick T. Kiley; Nellie Law, *Air Force;* Roberta Leighton, Harcourt Brace Jovanovich; Col. Henry F. Lippincott; Anton C. Massin, University of Notre Dame Library; William Matheson, Library of Congress; Carol Meyer, Harcourt Brace Jovanovich; Prof. Michael Millgate, University of Toronto; Jack H. Mooney, *Air University Review;* Julian Muller, Harcourt Brace Jovanovich; Col. John H. Napier III; National Library of Australia; Edward Newhouse; Harriet Oglesbee, Cooper Library; Prof. James A. Parrish, Jr., University of South Florida; Joseph Rees, Duke University Library; Anthony Rota, Bertram Rota Ltd.; John Bennett Shaw; Al Silverman, Book-of-the-Month Club; Sidney N. Towle, Headmaster, Kent School; Rita Vaughan, Harcourt Brace Jovanovich; Capt. John Vermillion, U. S. Military Academy; and Joyce Werner, Cooper Library. I have great debts to the staff of the Special Collections Department at the Princeton University Library: Charles E. Greene, Prof. Richard Ludwig, Mardel Pacheco, Jean F. Preston, Barbara Taylor, and Ann Van Arsdale. The University of South Carolina generously makes it possible for me to get my work done: I am particularly obligated to former Provost Keith Davis for a Shell travel grant and to Prof. George Geckle, Chairman of the Department of English.

Meredith Walker and Susan Walker typed and retyped this bibliography. The textual collations were prepared by Inge Kutt and Carol Johnston. Mrs. Johnston prepared the index. Richard Taylor did the photographic work.

It will be obvious to anyone familiar with the record of Cozzens scholarship that I am in debt to the work of my old friend Prof. James B. Meriwether. This bibliography builds on his *James Gould Cozzens: A Checklist* (1972).

James Gould Cozzens gave this bibliography his amazed approval and patient help. He supplied me with several of the English editions and provided information about his Air Force publications.

My working draft was vetted by William Cagle, Charles Mann, and Joel Myerson—all of whom improved it. I am grateful to Louise Craft of the University of Pittsburgh Press for giving the typescript its final editing. Ms.

Craft has improved every volume that she worked on, and she has saved me from many blunders. The Pittsburgh Series in Bibliography owes much to her hard labors. Frederick A. Hetzel, Director of the Press, has made this series possible.

Introduction

PUBLICATION is the essential act of scholarship, but all bibliographies are works in progress.

FORMAT

Section A lists chronologically all books and pamphlets by James Gould Cozzens, including all printings of all editions in English. The numbering system for Section A designates the edition and printing for each entry. Thus for the first English edition of *S. S. San Pedro*, *A7.2.a* indicates that the volume described is the seventh book by James Gould Cozzens *(A7)* and that it is the second edition, first printing *(2.a)*. Issues are designated by asterisks: *A6.1.a** indicates the English issue of the first printing of *Son of Perdition*. States are designated by inferior numbers: *A16.1.a₁* indicates the first state of the first printing of *By Love Possessed*. Section AA lists chronologically volumes revised or edited by Cozzens for which he did not receive title-page credit.

Section B lists chronologically all books and pamphlets in which material by Cozzens appeared for the first time. Previously unpublished items are so stipulated. The first printings only of these items are described.

Section C lists chronologically the first appearances of all Cozzens contributions in periodicals.

Section CC lists chronologically the unsigned contributions to the *Kent School News* and the *Kent Quarterly* that can be attributed to Cozzens.

Section D lists appearances of Cozzens manuscript material in booksellers' or auction catalogues.

Section E lists translations of Cozzens' books. His works are given alphabetically; the translations of each work, chronologically. No attempt has been made to follow rules of capitalization of foreign titles; these appear in all capital letters.

Appendix 1 lists movies made from Cozzens' works.

Appendix 2 contains the compiler's notes.

Appendix 3 lists books and pamphlets about Cozzens.

TERMS AND METHODS

Edition. All the copies of a book printed from a single setting of type—including all reprintings from standing type, from plates, or by photo-offset processes.

Printing. All the copies of a book printed at one time (without removing the type or plates from the press).

States. States occur only within single printings and are created by an alteration not affecting the conditions of issue to *some* copies of a given printing (by stop-press correction or cancellation of leaves). States appear in the first printing of *By Love Possessed* (A 16).

Issues. Issues occur only within single printings and are created by an alteration affecting the conditions of publication or sale to *some* copies of a given printing (usually a title-page alteration). Issues occur in *Son of Perdition* (A 6) and *A Cure of Flesh* (A 8).

Edition, printing, state, and *issue* have been restricted to the sheets of the books. Binding or dust-jacket variants have no bearing on these terms;[1] they are treated simply as binding or jacket variants.

State and *issue* are the most abused terms in the vocabulary of bibliographical description. Many cataloguers use them interchangeably as well as ignorantly. Much would be gained for the profession of bibliography by the consistent and precise usage of these terms.[2]

Dust jackets for Section A entries have been described in detail because they are part of the original publication effort and sometimes provide information about how the book was marketed. There is, of course, no certainty that a jacket now on a copy of a book was always on it.

For binding-cloth descriptions I have used the method proposed by G. Thomas Tanselle;[3] most of these cloth grains are illustrated in Jacob Blanck, ed., *The Bibliography of American Literature* (New Haven: Yale University Press, 1955–).

Color specifications are taken from the *ISCC-NBS Color-Name Charts Illustarted with Centroid Colors* (National Bureau of Standards).[4] In the descriptions of title pages, bindings, and dust jackets, the color of the lettering is

---

1. This statement holds for twentieth-century publishing. It is not possible to be so dogmatic for nineteenth-century publishing, when parts of a printing were marketed in different formats—for example, cloth, paper, and two-in-one bindings. In such cases it is difficult to avoid regarding the different bindings as issues because they do represent a deliberate attempt to alter the conditions of publication.

2. It was the hope of the general editor that the example of the Pittsburgh Series in Bibliography would encourage accurate application of bibliographical terms, but the hope seems forlorn. A recent guide to book-collecting offers this definition of *issue:* "Generally synonymous today with 'state,' referring to the priority of copies within the first edition, if indeed any priorities exist. The earliest copies released are known as the first issue. While sometimes it is a matter of varying colors or types of binding (or even in rare cases of the type of paper on which the book has been printed), issues are generally created by errors that may be corrected during the press run." There are five errors or inaccuracies in this explanation: (1) *Issue* is not synonymous with *state.* (2) *Issues* and *states* occur only within printings. (3) The earliest copies released are not known as the first issue unless there is a second issue. (4) Issue is not determined by binding or paper (except in the unlikely case of paper change during the press run of a single printing). (5) Stop-press correction of the type or plates during the run of a printing may create *issues* or *states,* depending on the nature of the alteration.

3. G. Thomas Tanselle, "The Specifications of Binding Cloth," *The Library,* 21 (September 1966), 246–247.

4. See G. Thomas Tenselle, "A System of Color Identification for Bibliographical Description," *Studies in Bibliography,* 20 (1967), 203–234.

always black, unless otherwise stipulated. A color holds for subsequent lines until a color change is stipulated. The style of type is roman, unless otherwise stipulated.

The spines of bindings and dust jackets are printed horizontally unless otherwise stipulated.

The term *perfect binding* refers to books in which the pages are held together with adhesive along the back edge after the folds have been trimmed off—for example, most paperbacks.

The locations rubric does not list every copy examined.

Dates provided within brackets do not appear on the title pages. Usually—but not invariably—they are taken from the copyright pages.

James Gould Cozzens was concerned with improving his work as long as it remained in print; he revised his books when new editions were being set. This bibliography includes textual collations of the first American edition against the first English edition and of the first American edition against the latest American edition. In the latter cases the reader should understand that all Cozzens' revisions did not necessarily appear at the same time. It is necessary to spot-check intermediate editions or printings in order to identify the stage when a particular revision first appeared in print. The collations printed here list substantive variants only. Since these lists are based on single collations, it is likely that multiple collations would yield more variants.

Locations are provided by the following symbols:

BL: British Library, London
LC: Library of Congress
Lilly: Lilly Library, Indiana University
MJB: Collection of Matthew J. Bruccoli
PSt: Pennsylvania State University Library

For paperbacks the serial number provided is that of the first printing. Paperback publishers normally change the serial number for later printings, but this information has not been noted.

It is desirable in bibliographical descriptions to avoid end-of-line hyphens in transcriptions. Because of word lengths and a measured line, however, it is impossible to satisfy this requirement in every case. End-of-line hyphens have been avoided wherever possible, and always where a hyphen would create ambiguity.

A bibliography is outdated the day it goes to the printer. Addenda and corrigenda are earnestly solicited.

The University of South Carolina
19 March 1979

A. Separate Publications

A 1 A DEMOCRATIC SCHOOL
Only printing (1920)

Reprint from

THE

ATLANTIC

MONTHLY

MARCH, 1920

A 1: 8½″ × 4⅜″

[1–6]

Single leaf folded twice.

Contents: p. 1: title; p. 2: statement by Kent Building Fund Campaign Committee; pp. 3–6: text. See C 3.

Typography and paper: 4″ × 8⁷⁄₁₆″. 41 lines per page. No running heads. Off-white wove paper.

Publication: Unknown number of copies distributed gratis in 1920.

Printing: Unknown.

Locations: Kent School, MJB.

A 2 CONFUSION
Only printing (1924)

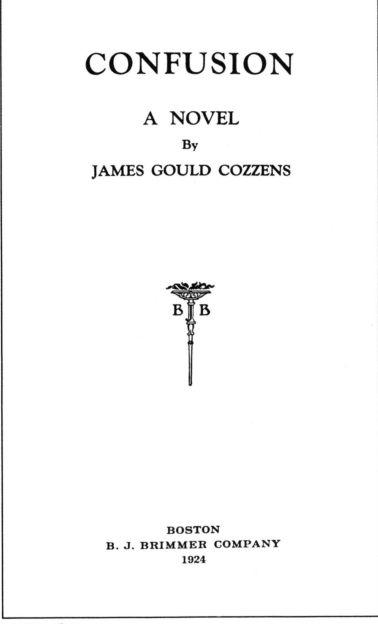

CONFUSION

A NOVEL

By

JAMES GOULD COZZENS

BOSTON
B. J. BRIMMER COMPANY
1924

A2: 7¼" × 4¹⁵⁄₁₆"

Copyright 1924
By B. J. BRIMMER COMPANY

First Printing, February, 1924

Press of
GOODMAN BROS., INC.
Boston, U. S. A.

[1–8] 9 [10] 11–37 [38] 39 [40–41] 42–109 [110] 111 [112–113] 114–145 [146–147] 148–175 [176] 177 [178] 179–215 [216] 217 [218] 219–263 [264] 265–295 [296] 297 [298] 299–345 [346] 347 [348] 349–389 [390] 391 [392] 393–404 [405–408]

[1–25]⁸ [26]⁴

Contents: p. 1: half title; p. 2: blank; p. 3: title; p. 4: copyright; p. 5: 'To | DOROTHEA'; p. 6: epigraph; p. 7: contents; p. 8: blank; p. 9: 'Part I | PIERRE D'ATREE'; p. 10: blank; pp. 11–404: text, headed 'CONFUSION | I.'; pp. 405–408: blank.

Typography and paper: 5½″ (5⅞″) × 3½″. 33 lines per page. Running heads: rectos and versos, 'CONFUSION'. Laid paper with vertical chain lines.

Binding: Goldstamped pale green (#149) B cloth (linen). Front: 'CONFUSION | [rule] | JAMES GOULD COZZENS'. Spine: 'CONFUSION | [double rules] | COZZENS | [BJB torch device] | BRIMMER'. Purple on white heraldic endpapers. All edges trimmed. Top edge stained dark red. Noted in blue remainder binding; these copies have the top edge unstained and lack the publisher's device and name on the spine: 'CONFUSION | [double rules] | COZZENS'. Also reported in brown remainder binding, but not seen.

Dust jacket: Front divided into red and purple triangles: '[white] CONFUSION | [rule] | JAMES GOULD COZZENS | THIS IS THE STORY OF | CERISE D'ATRÉE | THE DAUGHTER OF A | FRENCH FATHER AND | AN ENGLISH MOTHER | [coat of arms in white outlined in black] | B. J. Brimmer Company, Publishers, Boston'. Spine: '[against red] [white] CONFUSION | [rule] | COZZENS | [black] [BJB torch device] | BRIMMER'. Back: same as front, but with position of type and coat of arms reversed. Front flap: photo of Cozzens and biographical note. Back flap: blank.

Publication: Reported 2,000 copies of the only printing, of which 500 were remaindered. Published 3 April 1924. $2.00. Copyright #A 793983.

Printing: Printed by Goodman Bros., Boston, Mass. Bound by Union Bookbinding, Boston, Mass.

Locations: LC (JUL 12 '24, green); Lilly (green); MJB (green in dj; blue); PSt (green).

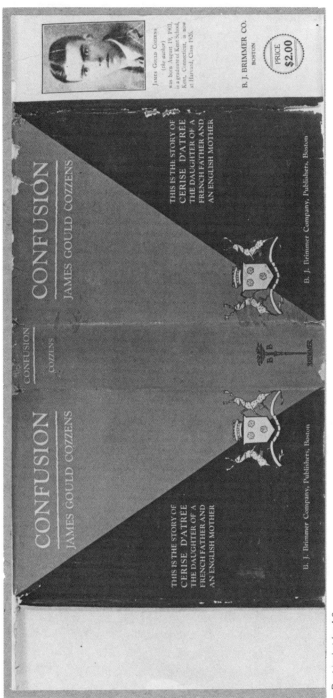

Dust jacket for A 2

A 3 THE CRITICISMS OF JOHN KEATS ON ENGLISH POETRY
Clothbound dummy (1925)

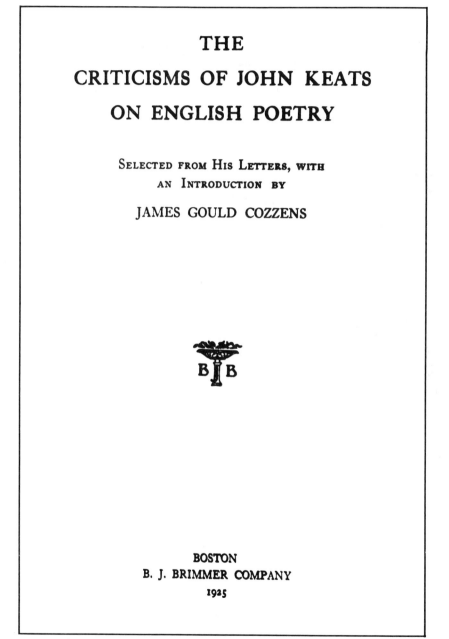

THE
CRITICISMS OF JOHN KEATS
ON ENGLISH POETRY

SELECTED FROM HIS LETTERS, WITH
AN INTRODUCTION BY

JAMES GOULD COZZENS

BⱵB

BOSTON
B. J. BRIMMER COMPANY
1925

A 3: 7″ × 3¹⁵⁄₁₆″

This book was not published. A unique dummy copy was in the collection of John Bennett Shaw, who donated it to the University of Notre Dame Library. Cozzens' "Preface" is reprinted in B 26.

[1–7] 8 [9] 10–11 [12–16]

[1]⁸

Contents: p. 1: half title; p. 2: *'THE IMPERISHABLE BOOKS'* [4 titles]; p. 3: title; p. 4: 'Copyright, 1925 | BY B. J. BRIMMER COMPANY | *Printed in the United States of America*'; p. 5: epigraph from Albert Elmer Hancock; p. 6: blank; pp. 7–8: 'PREFACE'; pp. 9–11: text; pp. 12–16: blank.

A 4 MICHAEL SCARLETT

A 4.1
First edition, only printing (1925)

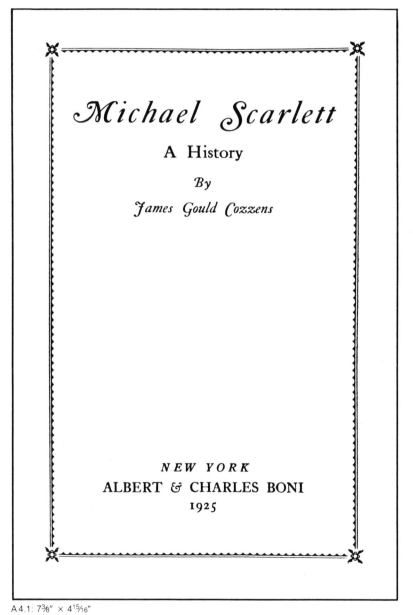

Michael Scarlett

A History

By

James Gould Cozzens

NEW YORK
ALBERT & CHARLES BONI
1925

A 4.1: 7⅜" × 4¹⁵⁄₁₆"

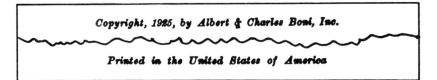

[1–10] 11–31 [32–34] 35–58 [59–60] 61–79 [80–82] 83–102 [103–104] 105–119 [120–122] 123–148 [149–150] 151–171 [172–174] 175–189 [190–192] 193–211 [212–214] 215–228 [229–230] 231–246 [247–248] 249–272 [273–274] 275–290 [291–292] 293–304 [305–306] 307–318 [319–320]

[1–20]⁸

Contents: p. 1: half title and epigraph; p. 2: blank; p. 3: title; p. 4: copyright; p. 5: 16-line dedication to Miss Wilifred White (see collation, A 4.2); p. 6: blank; p. 7: contents; p. 8: blank; p. 9: '*I: THE EXQUISITE YOUTH*'; p. 10: blank; pp. 11–318: text, headed '*Michael Scarlett* | A History | *CHAPTER I* | THE EXQUISITE YOUTH'; pp. 319–320: blank.

Typography and paper: 5¼" (5⁹⁄₁₆") × 3½". 29 lines per page. Running heads: rectos, chapter titles; versos, '*MICHAEL SCARLETT*'. Wove paper.

Binding: Black V cloth (smooth) stamped in orange. Front: '[within single-rule frame] MICHAEL SCARLETT | [leaf] | JAMES GOULD COZZENS'. Spine: 'Michael | Scarlett | [leaf] | James | Gould | Cozzens | Albert & | Charles Boni'. Off-white sized wove endpapers. All edges trimmed. Top edge stained orange.

Dust jacket: Printed on white. Front: '[within single-rule black frame] [black outlined in yellow] MICHAEL | SCARLETT | [black] BY JAMES | GOULD | COZZENS | [illustration in red, black, and yellow of man in Elizabethan dress, signed 'SB']'. Spine '[red] MICHAEL | SCARLETT | [black] [rule] | JAMES | GOULD | COZZENS | [red] ALBERT AND | CHARLES BONI'. Back: '[printed in red and black] MICHAEL | SCARLETT | *By* | JAMES GOULD COZZENS | [16-line blurb] | ALBERT & CHARLES BONI'. Front flap: biographical note on Cozzens and 4 excerpts from *Confusion* reviews. Back flap lists 6 Boni books.

Publication: Unknown number of copies. Published 2 November 1925. $2.00. Copyright #A 875002. The records of Brandt & Brandt, Cozzens' agent, indicate that 707 copies were sold.

Printing: Printed by Van Rees Press, New York. Bound by H. Wolff, New York.

Locations: BL (25 NOV '25); LC (NOV 11 '25); Lilly (dj); MJB (dj); PSt.

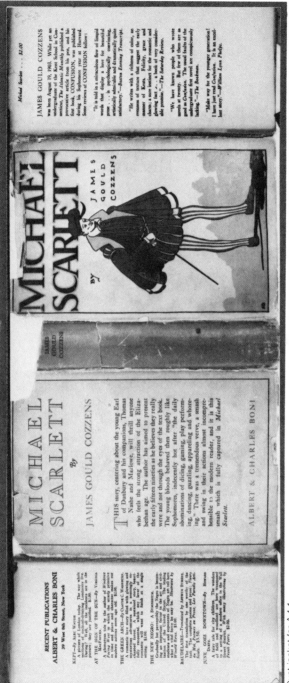

Dust jacket for A 4.1

A 4.2
English edition, only printing (1927)

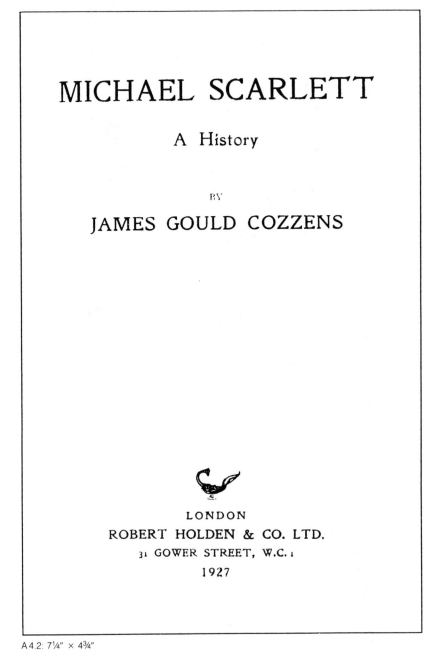

MICHAEL SCARLETT

A History

BY

JAMES GOULD COZZENS

LONDON
ROBERT HOLDEN & CO. LTD.
31 GOWER STREET, W.C. 1
1927

A 4.2: 7¼″ × 4¾″

[1–4] 5 [6] 7 [8] 9 [10] 11–31 [32–34] 35–59 [60] 61–80 [81–82] 83–103 [104] 105– 121 [122] 123–149 [150] 151–171 [172] 173 [174] 175–189 [190] 191 [192] 193–211 [212] 213 [214] 215–229 [230] 231–247 [248] 249–272 [273–274] 275–291 [292] 293–304 [305–306] 307–318 [319–320]

[1] 2–20⁸

Contents: p. 1: half title; p. 2: blank; p. 3: title; p. 4: copyright; p. 5: epigraph; p. 6: blank; p. 7: contents; p. 8: blank; p. 9: 'I: THE EXQUISITE YOUTH'; p. 10: blank; pp. 11–318: text, headed 'Michael Scarlett | A History | CHAPTER 1 | THE EXQUISITE YOUTH'; pp. 319–320: blank. At bottom of p. 318: 'FREDERICTON, NEW BRUNSWICK, 1924. | BERLIN, 1927.'

Typography and paper: 5⅜″ (5¾″) × 3½″. 29 lines per page. Same running heads as Boni printing. Wove paper.

Binding: Goldstamped strong red (#12) V cloth (smooth). Front has lamp in lower right. Spine: '[on gray panel within single-rule gold frame] *MICHAEL* | *SCARLETT* | [leaf] | *JAMES GOULD* | *COZZENS* | [below panel] *HOLDEN*'. Also noted in deep red (#13) V cloth with spine lettered in black, without lamp on front cover. White wove endpapers. All edges trimmed.

Dust jacket: Printed on yellowish brown. Front: '[red] MICHAEL | SCARLETT | [red, black, and blue illustration of 2 swordsmen in Elizabethan dress with third man down, signed 'E. J. I. A'] | [red] JAMES GOULD COZZENS'. Spine: '[black] MICHAEL | SCARLETT | JAMES | GOULD | COZZENS | [lamp] | HOLDEN'. Back: 'OTHER FICTION [7 titles]'. Front flap: blurb for *MS*. Back flap: blurb for *The Death Watch*.

Publication: Unknown number of copies of the only English printing. Published 23 June 1927. 7/6. The records of the A. M. Heath Co., Cozzens' English agent, indicate that 269 copies were sold.

Printing: See copyright page.

Locations: BL (goldstamped—23 JUN 27); Lilly (goldstamped in dj); MJB (black lettering in dj and goldstamped).

Collation: Substantive variants between the first American edition and the first English edition:

Boni (1925)		Holden (1927)	
1.4	*cunctarierbante*	[5.3	*cunctarierante*
5	MICHAEL SCARLETT	[	[dedication omitted]
	HIS HISTORY		
	BOTH WITH HOMAGE,		
	AND WITH		
	ADMIRATION AND ES-		
	TEEM		
	TO		
	MISS WILIFRED WHITE		
	MADAM:		
	I call on you thus long		
	after his inception to read		

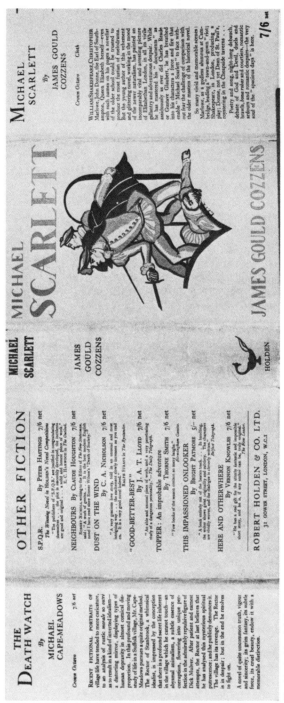

Dust jacket for A4.2

and I hope countenance
Michael Scarlett. Did I not
think him close to your wit,
that was his true begetter, I
had taught him a less am-
bition than to wear your
name. Now he approach-
eth your censure, tricked
with that care and skill I
had, content shall any
worth commend him, you
will count it yours and cast
the bye away
                    yours also,
                              J. G. C.

19.13	swords-play	[	19.13	sword-play
27.15–16	bowing. [no paragraph] Michael	[	27.16–17	bowing. [paragraph] Michael
40.7	Plautius	[	40.7	Plautus
45.5	Flooden	[	45.1	Flodden
66.2–3	Ambassadors'	[	66.3–4	Ambassador
67.28	but I think he	[	67.29	but he
70.14	[paragraph] "Quoth	[	70.15	[no paragraph] "Quoth
70.16	[paragraph] " 'Aye,'	[	70.16	[no paragraph] 'Aye,'
70.19	[paragraph] "Cried	[	70.19	[no paragraph] Cried
70.20	[no paragraph] Southampton	[	70.21	[paragraph] Southampton
79.3	Chester	[	79.6	Say
89.17	Good less-devil	[	89.19	Godless devil
95.26–27	I'd post to London and never leave, nor tutor	[	95.27–28	I'd be in London yet, nor ever have returned to tutor
95.27	Christspirit's another day."	[	95.28–29	Christspirit's."
96.21–22	that, since London was grown hot, I came back here where I scholared at Benet, called	[	96.22–24	that, London grown hot, I returned here, where once I scholared, no older than you, at Benet, called
102.12–14	hell. Maledicat Dominum, Christum, Virginem Beatem Mariam, Sanctos Apostolos Petrum et Paulum et omnen Sanctes, et te, fratrem! Hast	[	102.14–16	hell! Deus, Christus, Virgo Beata Maria, Sancti Apostoli Petrus Paulusque, Onmes Sanctique, et tu, frater; Maledicantur! Hast
113.20	alarums	[	113.20	alarms
119.30	Fox & Bolt	[	120.4	Fox and Bolt
127.28	tonight?	[	127.28	to-night.
129.16	frustrate	[	129.16	frustrated
130.4	*"His manus ob*	[	130.4	*"Ob*
130.4	*passi*	[	130.5	*passus*
133.26	Germane's	[	134.1	Germaine's
134.1–2	Puritan in everything but sentiment than Harvey.	[	134.5–6	Puritan than Harvey in everything but sentiment.
134.12	Cross & Keys [9 cases]	[	134.16–17	Cross and Keys [9 cases]
143.13	flundered	[	143.20	floundered
149	*THE VEIL OF NIGHT*	[	149	THE "VEIL OF NIGHT"

151	THE VEIL OF NIGHT	[	151	THE "VEIL OF NIGHT"
153.2–3	And a good	[	153.2–3	It was a good
153.5–8	play. Well formed verse, excellent nice songs, a pleasant story. Save Marlowe's Jew, the season's best, comic or tragic, thought Mr. Shakespere.	[	153.5–9	play. If it was disjointed now and now, small wonder, from the number of fingers in it besides my lord's. Its interest depended most slightly on its excellence, thought Mr. Shakespere.
154.23–24	Brave, nodded Mr. Shakespere, tapping the iambics.	[	154.24–25	"Hump," grunted Mr. Shakespere, "a prick from sirrah Marlowe."
155.21	can't	[	155.20	could not
156.21	apostrophied	[	156.18	apostrophised
157.5–7	Shakespere, "that's a piece for them! I do rate his young lordship high among our inventors."	[	157.1–2	Shakespere, "Byrd hath vastly helped my lord's lyric."
158.12–13	ill, if such change produced this piece. He's	[	158.7	ill. My lord's play hath pleasing parts. He's
158.13–14	yet, and raw, but he might go far."	[	158.8	yet."
169.16	monk's foot	[	169.11	monk's-hood
169.17	monk's foot	[	169.12	monk's-hood
173	*I' MI TRAVAI UN DI . . .*	[	173	OLIVES OF ENDLESS AGE
175	I' MI TRAVAI UN DI . . .	[	175	OLIVES OF ENDLESS AGE
176.1–2	comedy, called a 'Winter's Tale,' which, I do confess, doth	[	176.1–2	comedy, not produced yet, nor is it like to be soon now. It doth
180.5	or	[	180.6	of
181.20	arose	[	181.21	rose
183.2–3	unrushed	[	183.4–5	unbrushed
199.21–22	caring when the bolt's shot, canst credit affection beyond a high moment?"	[	199.26	caring past a point——"
203.21–25	expect? She led him. We struck at the plot's height. She was bewitching him with pants and signs. Aye, 'tis done now. An you're loyal, you'll ask a boy to shield England from her foes."	[	203.23	expect?
206.24	Nay	[	206.20	Hay
208.15	Jonson,	[	208.8	Jonson.
210.7	whipt	[	210.1	whipped
220.22	Mend	[	220.20	Mind
223.21–24	leaper. Already he hath bedded me of a rat, yet ceaseth not to abuse me. Out, you gull, you goose cap! Lay on't!"	[	223.20	leaper.

224.8–11	withal. [paragraph] "Stay, my beauty," cried Greene, "prithee clothe thyself." [paragraph] "To what end? I'm as soon undone."	[	224.4	withal.
224.15–18	leystall!" called one. "A ducat for thy virginity," shouted another. "Prithee where dost keep it, sweet Cynthia?"	[	224.9	leystall!"
239.9	[no paragraph] "This	[	239.9	[paragraph] "This
243.2	an	[	242.28	a
251.11	syllibant	[	251.11	sibilant
263.1–5	eyes. [paragraph] "Zounds, thou'lt set her raving after God," muttered Nashe thickly. "She's so seized now and now." [paragraph] "Yet I will praise God—" said Peg. [paragraph] Marlowe arose roaring to his feet.	[	263.1	eyes.
264.8	boat?" he asked	[	264.4	boat?"
269.17–20	dark." [paragraph] "The Lord is thy keeper: the Lord is thy shade upon thy right hand," whined the old man from the corner.	[	269.15	dark."
286.1	mutability	[	286.1	faithlessness
288.25–26	but never moved. [paragraph] "Thou'lt	[	288.26	but did not move. [no paragraph] "Thou'lt
295.22	dirk. [no paragraph] "This	[	295.22–23	dirk. [paragraph] "This
298.7–8	never budged	[	298.8–9	did not budge
300.11	and	[	300.11	an
301.3	Legs!	[	301.3	Kegs!
312.20	saw	[	312.20	realised
318.24	THE END	[		[omitted]

A 5 COCK PIT

A 5.1.a
Only edition, first printing (1928)

A 5.1.a: 7^{7}/$_{16}$″ × 5^{1}/$_{16}$″

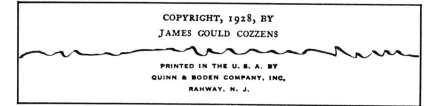

COPYRIGHT, 1928, BY
JAMES GOULD COZZENS

PRINTED IN THE U. S. A. BY
QUINN & BODEN COMPANY, INC.
RAHWAY, N. J.

[i–xii] 1–119 [120–122] 123–231 [232–234] 235–302 [303–304]

[1–19]⁸ [20]⁶

Contents: pp. i–ii: blank; p. iii: half title; p. iv: blank; p. v: title; p. vi: copyright; p. vii: 'To | Mr. and Mrs. Joseph Eggleston | in the happy memory | of Tuinucú'; p. viii: blank; p. ix: contents; p. x: blank; p. xi:' I | *THE CANE*'; p. xii: blank; pp. 1–302: text, headed '•1•'; pp. 303–304: blank.

Typography and paper: 5¼" (5¾") × 3⁵⁄₁₆". 29 lines per page. Running heads: rectos and versos, 'COCK PIT'. Wove paper.

Binding: Black V cloth (smooth) stamped in orange. Front: '[all within blindstamped single-rule frame] [within decorated frame] COCK PIT | [wavy rule] | James Gould Cozzens'. Spine: '[sawtooth rule] | COCK PIT | [wavy rule] | Cozzens | MORROW | [sawtooth rule]'. White map endpapers printed in orange. All edges trimmed. Top edge stained orange.

Dust jacket: Printed on light green. Front and spine have illustration of sugar cane and flames in orange, yellow, black, and green signed 'f. mechau'. Front: '[on light green panel] [yellow circle outlined in black] [black] COCK PIT [yellow circle outlined in black] | [on light green panel within single-rule black frame] [black] James Gould Cozzens | [below drawing, in orange on light green panel] *"Real plot, real people, real action, real excitement, | and the pure romantic feeling."* —GRANT OVERTON'. Spine: '[black on light green panel] COCK | PIT | [on light green panel] COZZENS | [below drawing on light green panel] MORROW'. Back: ads for 7 Morrow novels on yellow panel. Front flaps: blurbs for *CP* by Grant Overton and Ford Madox Ford. Back flap: 10 excerpts from *Confusion* reviews.

Publication: Unknown number of copies of the first printing. Published 20 September 1928. $2.50. Copyright #A 1053466. The Brandt & Brandt records indicate that 1,999 copies were sold, as well as 2,986 copies of a "special edition."

Printing: Printed and bound by Quinn & Boden, Rahway, N.J.

Locations: LC (SEP 22 1928); Lilly; MJB (dj); PSt.

Review copy: Bound copy with white slip printed in black inserted: '[type decoration] | *This book will* | *be published on* | [stamped] SEP 20 1928 | [printed]William Morrow & Co., Inc. | 386 Fourth Ave. New York'. *Location:* MJB.

A 5.1.b
Second printing: New York: Morrow, 1928.

On copyright page: 'First printing, September, 1928 | Second printing, September, 1928'.

Dust jacket for A 5.1.a

A 5.1.c
Third printing: New York: Grosset & Dunlap, [1933].

On copyright page: 'First printing, September, 1928 | Second printing, September, 1928'.

A 6 THE SON OF PERDITION

A 6.1.a
Only edition, first printing, first issue (1929)

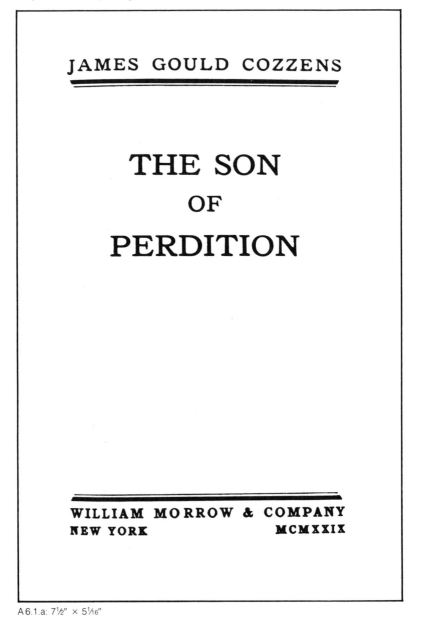

JAMES GOULD COZZENS

THE SON
OF
PERDITION

WILLIAM MORROW & COMPANY
NEW YORK   MCMXXIX

A 6.1.a: 7½″ × 5 1/16″

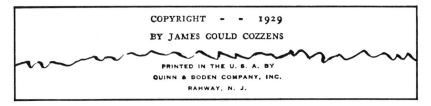

COPYRIGHT - - 1929

BY JAMES GOULD COZZENS

PRINTED IN THE U. S. A. BY
QUINN & BODEN COMPANY, INC.
RAHWAY, N. J.

[A–B] [i–vi] vii–viii [ix–x] [1–2] 3–304 [305–308]

[1–20]^8

Contents: pp. A–B: blank; p. i: half title and epigraph; p. ii: blank; p. iii: title; p. iv: copyright; p. v: 'FOR SYLVIA | *Outliving her beauty's outward, with a mind* | *That doth renew swifter than blood decays.*' p. vi: blank; pp. vii–viii: note: '*The United Sugar Company. . . . Joel B. Stellow.*'; p. ix: contents; p. x: blank; p. 1: half title; p. 2: blank; pp. 3–304: text, headed '————I———— | *MONO PASMADO'*; pp. 305–308: blank.

Typography and paper: 5¼" (5¾") × 3⁵⁄₁₆". 27 lines per page. Running heads: rectos and versos, 'THE SON OF PERDITION'. Wove paper.

Binding: Brilliant yellow (#83) V cloth (smooth). Front: '[within decorated frame] The SON of | PERDITION | [wavy rule] | James Gould Cozzens'. Spine: '[sawtooth rule] | The SON | of | PERDITION | [wavy rule] | Cozzens | MORROW | [sawtooth rule]'. Yellow endpapers with orange bird design. Top and bottom edges trimmed; fore-edge rough-trimmed. Top edge stained dark gray.

Dust jacket: Front and spine have illustration on yellow in green, red, purple, white, and blue of roof of USC loading terminal with train and ship—with light brown shadow profile of man's head. Front: '[blue] *The* SON *of* | PERDITION | JAMES GOULD COZZENS | AUTHOR OF "COCKPIT" '. Spine: '[blue] *The* | SON | *of* | PERDITION | JAMES | GOULD | COZZENS | [on white rectangle] MORROW'. Back: ads for 8 Morrow novels in yellow, blue, and white. Front and back flaps printed in blue. Front flap: blurb for *SOP*. Back flap: blurb for *On the Anvil*.

Publication: Unknown number of copies of the first printing. Published 22 August 1929. $2.50. Copyright #A 11821. The Brandt & Brandt records indicate that 1,979 copies were sold.

Printing: Printed and bound by Quinn & Boden, Rahway, N.J.

Locations: LC (AUG 24 1929); Lilly (dj); MJB (dj; 'OFFICE FILE COPY').

Dust jacket for A 6.1.a

A 6.1.a*
First edition, first printing, English issue (1929)

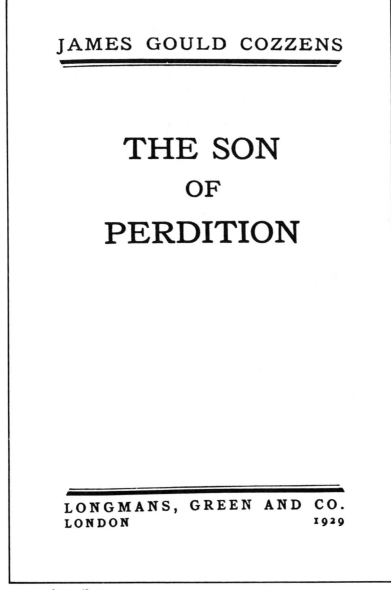

JAMES GOULD COZZENS

THE SON

OF

PERDITION

LONGMANS, GREEN AND CO.
LONDON   1929

A 6.1.a*: 7⅜″ × 4¹⁵⁄₁₆″

LONGMANS, GREEN AND CO. LTD.
39 Paternoster Row, London, E.C. 4
6 Old Court House Street, Calcutta
53 Nicol Road, Bombay
167 Mount Road, Madras

COPYRIGHT - - 1929

BY JAMES GOULD COZZENS

PRINTED IN THE U. S. A. BY
QUINN & BODEN COMPANY, INC.
RAHWAY, N. J.

Same pagination as Morrow issue.

Same collation as Morrow issue.

Contents: Same as Morrow issue. This issue consists of Morrow sheets with a new first gathering to provide the Longmans title page and copyright page.

Typography and paper: Same as Morrow issue.

Binding: Vivid reddish orange (#34) B cloth (linen). Front: 'THE | SON OF PERDITION | JAMES GOULD COZZENS'. Spine: 'THE | SON OF | PERDITION | J. G. | COZZENS | LONGMANS'. White wove endpapers. All edges trimmed.

Dust jacket: Not seen.

Publication: 1,000 sets of the Morrow sheets were imported by Longmans. Published 3 October 1929. 7/6. The A. M. Heath records indicate that 222 copies were sold. There were probably cheap or remainder copies.

Printing: See copyright page.

Locations: BL (10 OCT 29); MJB.

A 6.1.b
Second printing: London: Longmans, Green, 1931.

Not seen. The Longmans records indicate that 750 copies were bound. The A. M. Heath records indicate that 692 copies were sold. This may not have been a new printing, but a binding of English-issue sheets with new title leaf.

A 6.1.c
Third printing: New York: Grosset & Dunlap, [1933].

A 6.1.d
Fourth printing: Cleveland: World, 1942.

Not seen. 10,000 copies.

A 6.1.e
Fifth printing: Cleveland & New York: World, [1943].

On copyright page: 'SECOND PRINTING MAY 1943'.

4,710 copies.

Note: A dramatization of *The Son of Perdition* by Lynn Riggs premiered at the Hedgerow Theatre, Moylan-Rose Valley, Pa., 25 February 1933.

A 7 S.S. SAN PEDRO

A 7.1
First edition, only printing [1931]

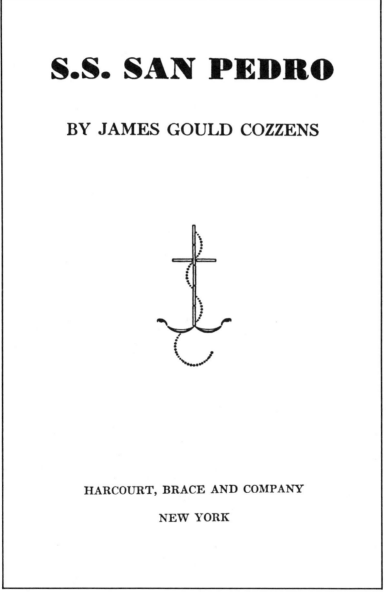

S.S. SAN PEDRO

BY JAMES GOULD COZZENS

HARCOURT, BRACE AND COMPANY

NEW YORK

A 7.1: 7⅜″ × 4¹⁵⁄₁₆″

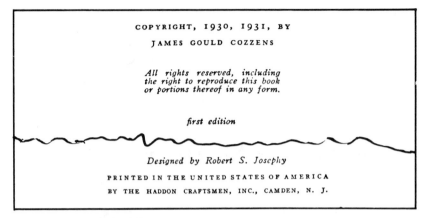

[i–vi] [1–2] 3–136 [137–138]

[1–9]^8

Contents: p. i: half title; p. ii: blank; p. iii: title; p. iv: copyright; p. v: *'For my Mother in memory of | Nova Scotia sea captains'*; p. vi: blank; p. 1: half title; p. 2: blank; pp. 3–136: text, headed 'S.S. SAN PEDRO | [ornaments]'; pp. 137–138: blank.

Typography and paper: 5³⁄₁₆″ (5¹¹⁄₁₆″) × 3½″. 21 lines per page. Running heads: rectos and versos, 'S.S. SAN PEDRO'. Wove paper.

Binding: Silverstamped grayish green (#150) or grayish blue (#186) V cloth (smooth). Front has anchor and rope. Spine: '[horizontal] *cozzens* | [vertical] S.S. SAN PEDRO | [horizontal] HARCOURT | BRACE | AND | CO.' White wove endpapers. All edges trimmed.

Dust jacket: Front and spine have illustration of sinking ship and lifeboats in red, green, black, and white, signed 'ETT'. Front: '[on white panel between black and red rules] S.S. SAN PEDRO | [on white panel between black and red rules] [black] JAMES GOULD COZZENS'. Spine: '[on white panel within black and red rules] S.S. | San | Pedro | *Cozzens*'. Back: ads for *The Waves* and 5 other books. Front and back flaps printed in green and black. Front flap: blurb for *SSSP*. Back flap: blurb for *Sleuths*. Variation has been noted in the front dust jacket illustration: the sea, sky, and ship are in different shades of green—very light green (#143) or very light bluish green (#162).

Publication: 10,500 copies of the first printing. Published 27 August 1931. $1.50. Copyright #A 43350. The Brandt & Brandt records indicate that 4,446 copies of the trade printing were sold.

Printing: Printed and bound by Haddon Craftsmen, Camden, N.J.

Locations: LC (AUG 31 1931; both copies green); Lilly (blue cloth in dj); MJB (green and blue cloth; both in dj); PSt (blue cloth in dj).

Note 1:   *S.S. San Pedro* was the August 1931 Book-of-the-Month Club selection. It has been assumed that the blue bindings are BOMC copies, but the books are not differentiated in any way. It is possible that there are concealed printings among the copies bearing the *'first edition'* slug.

Note 2:   This work was first published as "S.S. 'San Pedro' A Tale of the Sea," *Scribner's Magazine*, LXXXVIII (August 1930) in the *Scribner's* short-novel contest. See C46.

S.S. SAN PEDRO

by James Gould Cozzens

One of the most unexpected and terrible disasters of recent years, the sinking of the S.S. Vestris, will be vividly remembered by all those who read this compact, mountainous tale. It tells how the S.S. San Pedro, an ocean liner bound from New York to the Argentine, with full cargo, a million dollars in gold, and a crowded list of holiday passengers, went down off the Atlantic coast. It is a relentless and dramatic story of the battle with the storm, the ship more and more powerless, the captain facing the fatal risk with stubborn courage. . . .

This short novel establishes James Gould Cozzens as one of the most effective and talented of modern story-tellers. Mr. Cozzens has succeeded as remarkably in this neglected form of fiction as he has in the more familiar field of the full-length novel. His books, "Cockpit" and "The Son of Perdition," are well known, and "S.S. San Pedro" was the first story to be published in the $2,000 prize contest conducted last year by Scribner's Magazine.

Harcourt, Brace and Company
383 MADISON AVENUE, NEW YORK

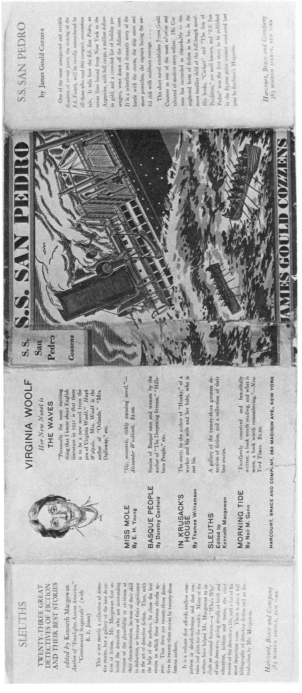

S.S. SAN PEDRO

S.S. San Pedro Cozzens

JAMES GOULD COZZENS

VIRGINIA WOOLF

Her New Novel is
THE WAVES

"Personally the most exciting thing that I know about English literature in 1931 is that there is to be a new novel from the pen of Virginia Woolf." *Hugh Walpole.* Mrs. Woolf is the author of "Orlando," "Mrs. Dalloway," etc.

"Sly, eccentric, richly amusing novel."—*Alexander Woollcott.* $2.00.

MISS MOLE
By E. H. Young

BASQUE PEOPLE
By Dorothy Canfield

Stories of Basque men and women by the author of "The Deepening Stream," "Hillsboro People," etc.

IN KRUSACK'S HOUSE
By Thames Williamson

The story, by the author of "Hunky," of a worker and his wife and her baby, who is not his.

SLEUTHS
Edited by Kenneth Macgowan

A gallery of the twenty-three greatest detectives of fiction, and a collection of their best stories.

MORNING TIDE
By Neil M. Gunn

"Excellently conceived and beautifully written, a book worth reading, and what is more, a book worth remembering."—*New York Times.* $2.50.

HARCOURT, BRACE AND COMP'NY, 383 MADISON AVE., NEW YORK

SLEUTHS

TWENTY-THREE GREAT DETECTIVES OF FICTION AND THEIR BEST STORIES

edited by Kenneth Macgowan
Author of "Footlights Across America," "Continental Stagecraft" (with R. E. Jones)

This is not merely a collection of detective stories, but a gallery of the best detectives of fiction. Mr. Macgowan first selected the detectives who are outstanding because of the plausibility or vividness of their characterization, because of their skill in deduction, or because of their significance in the art of detective fiction. Then, with the help of the authors, he chose the best stories in which these famous sleuths appear. Thus there are twenty-three detectives in twenty-three stories by twenty-three famous authors.

It is a volume that affords endless comparison in detective-technique and that contains real plots for the reader. Many of the authors have helped Mr. Macgowan to include an unusual feature,—a "Who's Who" of each detective, giving details of birth and education, hobbies and tastes, the chief events of the detective's life, and a list of his most important cases. There is also a full bibliography of detective fiction and an Introduction by Mr. Macgowan.

Harcourt, Brace and Company
383 MADISON AVENUE, NEW YORK

Dust jacket for A7.1

A 7.2.a
English edition, first printing (1931)

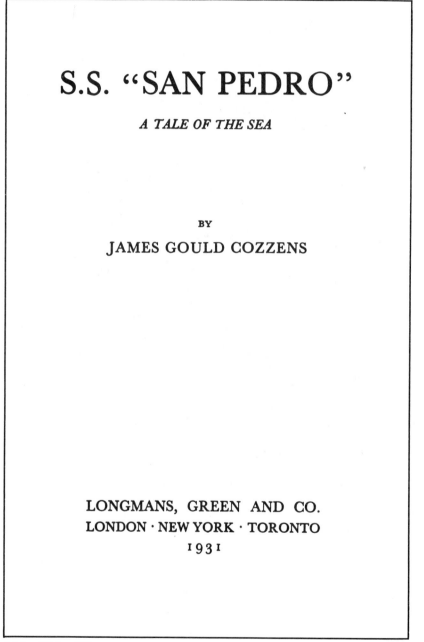

S.S. "SAN PEDRO"

A TALE OF THE SEA

BY

JAMES GOULD COZZENS

LONGMANS, GREEN AND CO.
LONDON · NEW YORK · TORONTO
1931

A 7.2.a: 7¹¹⁄₁₆″ × 5½″

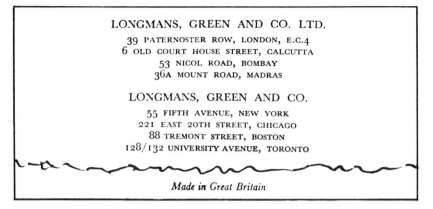

[1–8] 9–53 [54] 55–118 [119–120]

[A] B–G⁸ H⁴

Contents: pp. 1–2: blank; p. 3: half title; p. 4: '[within single-rule frame] *By the same Author* | THE SON OF PERDITION'; p. 5: title; p. 6: copyright; p. 7: dedication; p. 8: blank; pp. 9–119: text, headed 'S.S. "San Pedro" '; p. 120: *'Printed by* THE SHENVAL PRESS'.

Typography and paper: 5" (5½") × 3⁵⁄₁₆". 26 lines per page. Running heads: rectos and versos, 'S.S. "SAN PEDRO" '. Laid paper with vertical chain lines.

Binding: Dark greenish blue (#174) V cloth (smooth). Front has blindstamped single-rule frame. Spine goldstamped: '[rule] | S.S. | *San* | *Pedro* | [diamond] | *J. G.* | *Cozzens* | *Longmans* | [rule]'. Laid white endpapers. All edges trimmed. Top edge stained greenish blue.

Dust jacket: Front, spine, and back have repeated design of sinking black ships on green and light blue sea. Front: '[on light blue panel within single-rule black frame] *S.S. SAN PEDRO* | *A Tale of the Sea* | [ornament] | *J. G. COZZENS*'. Spine: '[on light blue panel within single-rule black frame] *S.S.* | *SAN* | *PEDRO* | *A Tale* | *of the* | *Sea* | [decoration] | *J. G.* | *Cozzens* | [on light blue panel within single-rule black frame] *LONGMANS*'. Front flap: excerpt from *SSSP* and price. Back flap: *'Made in Great Britain'*.

Publication: 2,000 copies of the first English printing. Published 10 September 1931. 6s. The A. M. Heath records indicate that 2,851 copies of the first and second printings were sold, and that 183 were remaindered in 1934.

Printing: Printed by the Shenval Press.

Locations: BL (18 SEP 31); Lilly (dj); MJB (dj).

Collation: Substantive variants between the first American edition and the first English edition:

Harcourt, Brace (1931)			Longmans, Green (1931)	
19.4	said when it was over.	[	22.13	said.
40.19	severe and noncommittal	[	40.15	severely non-committal
41.5–9	ear. His pointed young face turned, flippant in pro-	[	40.22	ear. "Plenty," he grunted.

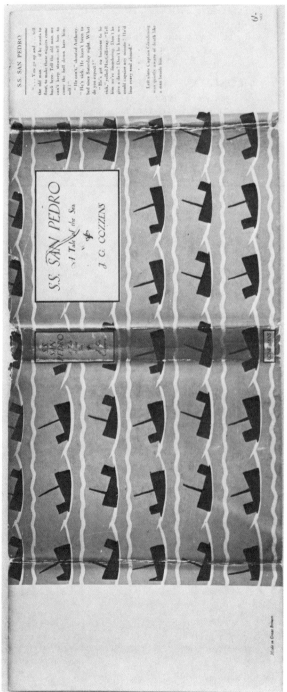

"... You go up and ... tell the old man ... if he wants to float, to make these tuggers come back here. Tell the old man we can't keep steam—tell him to come the hell down here himself!"

"He can't," shouted Anthony.

"He's sick. He hasn't been to bed since Saturday night. What do you expect?"

"He's got no business to be sick," yelled MacGillivray. "Tell him we're foundering. Don't be give a damn. Does he know, we could capsize any minute. He'd lose every soul aboard—"

Left alone Captain Clendening was quietly aware of death like a man beside him.

Made in Great Britain

S.S. SAN PEDRO
A Tale of the Sea
by
J. G. COZZENS

Dust jacket for A 7.2.a

file, suiting itself to the un-
original jargon of his ready
mockery. He spoke at
once, with the accent, jeer-
ing, tight-voweled, of poor
Boston streets. "Plenty,"
he said.

43.14	Mr. Mills.	[	42.19–20	The name proved to be Mills.
51.9	Above and behind him, the light cast	[	49.3	The light above and behind him cast
59.14–15	south," he said formally, "fourteen degrees east."	[	57.8–9	south fourteen degrees east," he said formally.
68.17	often and audibly	[	64.21	loudly and audibly
73.21– 74.1	aside." [paragraph] She	[	69.3–6	aside." [paragraph] "I don't know," she said, whiter still, "whether I'd rather have him really here, or have him not really here." She moistened her lips. [paragraph] "I've got to get aft," said Anthony. [paragraph] She
75.7	Morris, delighted, "but	[	70.9	Morris, "but
75.11–12	Morris. He drawled with rel-ish, gleeful, "These	[	70.13	Morris. "These
84.5	above	[	77.17	upstairs
101.18	now	[	91.17	this time
109.3–6	Morris. He hesitated an in-stant, examining the palms of his hands. Then he wiped them deliberately on the seams of his uniform trousers. "He	[	97.16	Morris. "He
109.12–13	now." His face stirred, be-came lively, grinning. "Pretty	[	97.23	now. Pretty
110.6	Morris, enlivened, "but	[	98.12	Morris, "but
119.17– 120.2	jolts; and jarred beyond endurance, he had to stop, putting a hand, somehow worked raw, against the wall. He might have slept a moment, on his feet, to his shins in cold water, for he started, almost falling; re-membered where he was going.	[	106.11	jolts.
123.15–16	him. "Wake up!" he roared. "Come to! You	[	109.11–12	him. "Not do you any good. You
124.1–2	boy? Are you all crazy? You	[	109.18	boy? You

125.19   brat! Believe   [111.5–6   brat! Take your play-acting
                                                            upstairs! Believe

A 7.2.b
Second English printing: London, New York & Toronto: Longmans, Green, 1931.

Not seen. The Longmans records show that 2,000 copies were printed.

A 7.2.c
Third English printing: London, New York & Toronto: Longmans, Green, 1934.

On copyright page: 'First Edition, September 1931. | Second Impression, September
1931. | Reissued in Swan Library, March 1934.'

Swan Library. #19. The A. M. Heath records indicate that 601 copies were sold.

A 7.3
Third edition: World's Great Tales of the Sea, ed. William McFee. Cleveland & New
York: World, [1944], pp. 186–234.

On copyright page: 'FORUM BOOKS EDITION | First Printing August 1944'.

A 7.4
Fourth edition: World's Great Tales of the Sea. New York: Editions for the Armed
Services, [1945].

#765.

Note: Republished in *The Seven Seas,* I (Winter 1953), 82–129.

A 7.5
Fifth edition: New York: Berkley, [1955].

#103. 25¢. Wrappers. Reprinted 1958.

A 7.6.a
Sixth edition, Modern Library: S.S. San Pedro and Castaway. New York: Random
House, [1956].

#P17. 95¢. Wrappers. 35,675 copies of the Modern Library/Vintage printings were sold
(see A 7.6.b and A 9.6). Reprinted February 1958 and October 1959.

A 7.6.b
Sixth edition, Vintage: S.S. San Pedro and Castaway. New York: Vintage, [1961].

#V-138. 95¢. Wrappers. Reprinted 1967.

A 7.7
Seventh edition: TODAY LIBRARY 75 | [underline] | JAMES GOULD COZZENS | S.S.
SAN PEDRO | WITH INTRODUCTION AND NOTES | BY TOSHIO EBIZUKA | YAMAGU-
CHI SHOTEN

Tokyo, 1965. Wrappers.

A 7.8.a
Eighth edition, first printing: New York: Harcourt, Brace & World, [1967].

"Uniform Edition." $3.50.

Collation: Substantive variants in the American editions:

Harcourt, Brace (1931)			Harcourt, Brace & World "Uniform Edition" (1967)	
v	*For my Mother in memory of Nova Scotia sea captains*	[		[dedication omitted]
14.11–12	weigh," he explained.	[	10.6	way," he said.
16.17–18	answered Anthony.	[	11.18	Anthony said.
20.9	powerful?" he inquired huskily. He	[	13.22	powerful?" He
26.11	weigh	[	17.12	way
29.3	[no paragraph] Thinking	[	19.18	[paragraph] Thinking
33.6	grunted	[	22.3	said
59.17	echoed	[	38.29	said
59.19	announced	[	39.1	said
62.3–4	requested	[	40.11	said
75.6	admitted	[	48.8	said
75.9	marveled	[	48.11	said
75.11	agreed	[	48.13	said
75.16	invited	[	48.17	said
75.19	grunted	[	48.20	said
76.3	urged	[	48.24	said
80.18	White	[	51.21	Livid
86.10–11	had below was	[	55.2	had was
88.21	snapped	[	56.15	said
92.11–12	eye, made her reach down and rouse him.	[	59.7	eye.
105.20	assented	[	67.10	said
109.20	boats. Well—"	[	69.21	boats."
110.18	admired	[	70.5	said
111.10	suggested	[	70.16	said
111.12	snapped	[	70.18	said
111.20	begged	[	70.24	said
112.5	applauded	[	70.30	said
112.10	claimed	[	71.4	said
112.20	nodded	[	71.12	said
116.18	requested	[	73.23	said
124.4	protested	[	78.4	said
132.7	nor	[	83.1	or

A 7.8.b

Eighth edition, Harvest printing: New York: Harcourt, Brace & World, [1968].

Harvest #HB135. $1.15. Wrappers.

A 7.8.c

Eighth edition, Longmans printing: [London]: Longmans, [1968].

The A. M. Heath records indicate that 1,811 copies were sold.

A 8 THE LAST ADAM

A 8.1.a
First edition, first printing [1933]

JAMES GOULD COZZENS

The Last Adam

HARCOURT, BRACE AND COMPANY

NEW YORK

A 8.1.a: 7^{15}/$_{16}$″ × 5^{3}/$_{8}$″

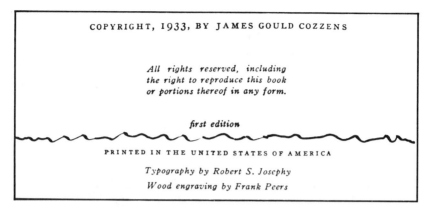

[i–vi] [1–2] 3–301 [302–306]

[1–19]⁸ [20]⁴

Contents: p. i: half title; p. ii: *'by the same author* | S.S. SAN PEDRO'; p. iii: title; p. iv: copyright; p. v: *With affectionate esteem* | *to Willard F. Read, M.D.'*; p. vi: blank; p. 1: half title; p. 2: blank; pp. 3–301: text, headed 'One'; pp. 302–306: blank.

Typography and paper: 5¹³⁄₁₆″ (6¼″) × 3⅝″. 32 lines per page. Runnings heads: rectos and versos, 'THE LAST ADAM'. Wove paper.

Binding: Dark gray (#266) buckram. Printed label on front with black-and-white illustration of country road, signed 'PEERS'. Spine: '[white] COZZENS | *The Last* | *Adam* | HARCOURT, BRACE | AND COMPANY'. White wove endpapers. All edges trimmed. Top edge stained light bluish green in some copies.

Dust jacket: Front and spine printed in white against black. Front: 'THE | LAST | ADAM | [white and red caduceus] | James Gould Cozzens'. Spine: 'THE | LAST | ADAM | COZZENS | Harcourt, Brace | and Company'. Back: photo of JGC with blurb for *SSSP*. Back and front flap printed in black and red. Front flap: blurb for *LA*. Back flap: blurb for *Pocahontas*. All examined copies lack the price on the front flap.

Publication: 10,000 copies of the first printing. Published 5 January 1933. $2.50. Copyright #A 57909.

Printing: Printed and bound by Vail-Ballou, Binghamton, N.Y.

Locations: BL (23 JAN '33); LC (JAN 13 1933); Lilly; MJB (dj; 3 copies); PSt.

Review copy: Bound copy with printed grayish green slip pasted to front flap of dust jacket: '[black] ADVANCE COPY | FROM HARCOURT, BRACE AND COMPANY | Please note the release date for review and the price | [stamped in dark gray] JAN 5 1933. $2 50'. *Location:* MJB.

Note: *The Last Adam* was the January 1933 Book-of-the-Month Club selection. Both the trade and the BOMC copies have the *'first edition'* slug on the copyright page. There is variation in the top-edge staining, and it is possible that the top edge in the BOMC copies is unstained.

A 8.1.b
Second printing: New York: Harcourt, Brace, [1933].

Dust jacket for A.8.1.a

On copyright page: 'Second printing, January, 1933'.

A front-cover ad in *Publishers Weekly,* CXXIII (21 January 1933), claims: "The first 10,000 were gone in ten days. The second 10,000 were ordered six days after publication. 5,000 more were ordered seven days after publication." The HBJ records indicate that the second printing was 6,000 copies and the third printing was 4,300 copies.

A8.1.c
Third printing: New York: Harcourt, Brace, 1933.

Not seen.

A8.1.d
Fourth printing: New York: Grosset & Dunlap, [1936].

On copyright page: 'Third printing, January, 1933'.

A8.1.e
Fifth printing: New York: Harcourt, Brace, [1956].

On copyright page: 'C.11.57'.

A 8.2.a
A Cure of Flesh
First English edition, first printing, first issue (1933)

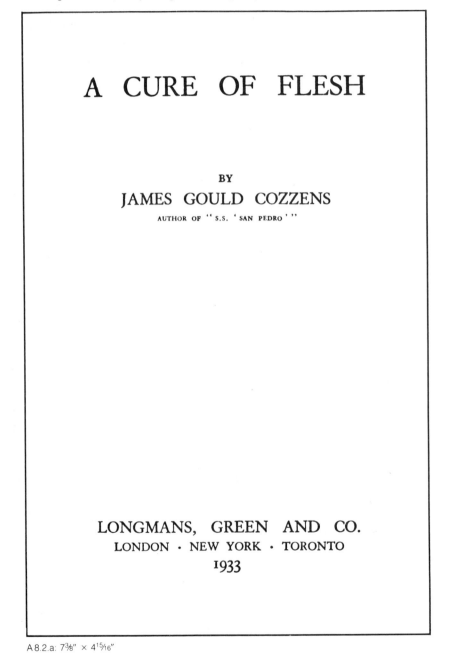

A CURE OF FLESH

BY

JAMES GOULD COZZENS

AUTHOR OF " S.S. ' SAN PEDRO ' "

LONGMANS, GREEN AND CO.

LONDON · NEW YORK · TORONTO

1933

A 8.2.a: 7⅜″ × 4¹⁵⁄₁₆″

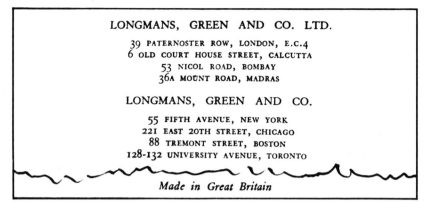

LONGMANS, GREEN AND CO. LTD.

39 PATERNOSTER ROW, LONDON, E.C.4
6 OLD COURT HOUSE STREET, CALCUTTA
53 NICOL ROAD, BOMBAY
36A MOUNT ROAD, MADRAS

LONGMANS, GREEN AND CO.

55 FIFTH AVENUE, NEW YORK
221 EAST 20TH STREET, CHICAGO
88 TREMONT STREET, BOSTON
128-132 UNIVERSITY AVENUE, TORONTO

Made in Great Britain

[1–4] 5–289 [290–292]

[A] B–I K–R^8 S^{10}

Contents: p. 1: half title; p. 2: books by JGC—lists *SSSP* and *SOP;* p. 3: title; p. 4: copyright; pp. 5–290: text, headed 'ONE | I'; pp. 291–292: blank.

Typography and paper: 5¼" (5⁹⁄₁₆") × 3½". 34 lines per page. Running heads: rectos and versos, 'A CURE OF FLESH'. Wove paper.

Binding: Deep reddish orange (#36) V cloth (smooth). Front: 'A CURE OF FLESH | JAMES | GOULD | COZZENS'. Spine: 'A CURE | OF | FLESH [decoration] | JAMES | GOULD | COZZENS | LONGMANS'. White wove endpapers. All edges trimmed.

Dust jacket: Printed on white. Front: '[red with black shadowing] A CURE | OF FLESH | [black, slanted up] A doctor's private life | is no concern . . . . . . | [red] JAMES GOULD COZZENS | [black] AUTHOR OF "S.S. SAN PEDRO" ETC.' Spine: 'A CURE | OF | FLESH | J. G. COZZENS | [within black and red single-rule frames] [black] A doctor's | private life | is no | concern . . . | [red Longmans ship device within oval] | [black] LONGMANS'. Back: 6 blurbs for *SSSP* in black and red. Front flap: price. Back flap blank.

Publication: 2,000 copies of the first English printing. Published 23 February 1933. 7/6. The A. M. Heath records indicate that 1,149 copies were sold.

Printing: P. 290: 'NORTHUMBERLAND PRESS LIMITED, NEWCASTLE UPON TYNE'.

Locations: BL (27 APR 33); MJB (dj).

Collation: Substantive variants between the first American edition of *The Last Adam* and the first English edition of *A Cure of Flesh:*

Harcourt, Brace (1933)			Longmans, Green (1933)	
v	*With affectionate esteem to*	[		[dedication omitted]
	Willard F. Read, M. D.			
9.18	would	[	11.11	had
12.2	littlest	[	13.25	least
22.15	mackinaw	[	23.18	mackintosh
45.2	chit-chat	[	45.13	chit and chat
45.9	by grasping firmly—	[	45.20	by firmly grasping the——
54.1	'70s	[	54.1	seventies

A CURE OF FLESH

J. G. COZZENS

A CURE OF FLESH

A doctor's private life . . . . . . is no concern . . .

A doctor's private life is no concern . . .

JAMES GOULD COZZENS
AUTHOR OF "S.S. SAN PEDRO" ETC.

LONGMANS

"One of the most vivid tales of the sea I have ever read."—ST. JOHN ERVINE.

S.S. SAN PEDRO

BY

JAMES GOULD COZZENS

GERALD GOULD in The Observer
"Mr. Cozzens reminds one vividly of Joseph Conrad. Humour, irony, tragedy, grandeur, are concentrated in this tiny space, and the wings of doom have infinite room to stretch in. The quality of the writing is astonishing."

RALPH STRAUS in The Sunday Times
"Told with a minimum of words but with real power and understanding. It certainly grips you. . . . Mr. Cozzens calls his book very simply 'a tale of the sea.' It is a very good tale."

Everyman
"Magnificently told in a fresh and modern way, but with all the overtones of the great tradition of the sea. . . . Mr. Cozzens has not only a brilliant style, but a vivid sense of character."

Morning Post
"A little masterpiece of the sea . . . . Comparison with Conrad it inevitable in such a case, but it is a comparison from which this young American writer emerges unscathed . . . an unforgettable little epic."

S. P. B. MAIS in The Daily Telegraph
"The quality of the writing is amazing. Once again, as in 'The Bridge of San Luis Rey,' Messrs. Longmans have got hold of a book that is different: one of those books that you will be wise to read at once, for everyone will be asking, 'Have you read S.S. San Pedro?' from now for at least a year."

Punch
"He resists admirably the temptation inherent in the theme to indulge in over-writing. And he is entirely free from that self-comparison, conscious or otherwise, with Conrad which is painfully evident in the work of nine out of ten novelists whose concern is with the sea . . . a brilliant and unforgettable piece of work, and Mr. Cozzens may be congratulated on having done a difficult thing with notable success."

6s. net

Dust jacket for A 8.2. a

61.1	had wet her drawers a little;	[	60.24	had lost control of herself;
76.26	Mr. Kean	[	75.23	Mr. Keen
80.31	effect	[	79.21	affect
81.5	effect	[	79.26	affect
85	[no section number]	[	83	1
93.27	sat	[	91.16	set
100.26	Bros.	[	98.7	Brothers
101.9	Bros.	[	98.18	Brothers
108.19	stop	[	105.23	step
110.8	slicker	[	107.8	raincoat
111.25	Register & Manual	[	108.25	Register and Manual
113.27	carefully. [no paragraph] "Come	[	110.24–25	carefully. [paragraph] "Come
114.30	ten dollar	[	111.24	ten-dollar
117.30–31	appearance'	[	114.19–20	appearance's
120.9	ten dollar	[	116.26	ten-dollar
124.20	slicker	[	120.31	raincoat
125.9	in	[	121.17	to
125.26–27	heap with their collected excrement, to be washed away together.	[	122.1–2	heap into the latrine to be washed away with its contents.
126.1	slicker	[	122.9	raincoat
134.27	coat room	[	130.25	cloakroom
134.32	coat room	[	130.30	cloakroom
138.4	he drive	[	133.34	he should drive
149.18	and Sunday	[	144.24	and on Sunday
152.21	neck."	[	147.30	neck and Larry climbing all over her."
152.32	is. You'd better keep your pants buttoned, Lester	[	148.9	is. You keep clear of women, Lester
153.1	you'll get yourself into trouble."	[	148.10	you'll work yourself up a good hot reinfection."
153.4–5	another	[	148.14–15	a catheter
153.25	pockets. [no paragraph] "That	[	148.34– 149.1	pockets. [new paragraph] "That
157.6	remorsely	[	152.9	remorselessly
157.21	you.	[	152.24	you?
165.10	towel	[	160.3	toilet
175.2	of women	[	169.11	of accommodating women
176	[no section number]	[	171	I
180.26	of	[	175.24	to
183.28	[section break]	[	178.21	[no section break]
192.6	else. If the feces aren't fluid, stir 'em up well."	[	186.16	else."
193.6	'90s	[	187.16	nineties
193.15	17th century	[	187.25	seventeenth-century
213.30	blame.	[	207.7	blame?
216.7	stealing	[	209.12	steeling
218.29	given	[	211.33	give
219.1–2	mackinaw	[	212.3–4	mackintosh
220.13	mackinaw	[	213.13	mackintosh

225.26	loose	[	218.21	lose
232.6	"She's only eight months gone."	[	224.16	"She isn't due for a month yet."
233.29	lightness	[	226.7	lightless
234.28	and, considering her kidneys, the	[	227.10	and the
236.20	in back	[	228.25–26	at the back
243.11	twelve hour shifts	[	235.15	twelve-hour shifts
252.2	curb	[	243.23	kerb
263.13	toward	[	254.18	towards
278.14	chasing	[	269.4	whoring
281	[no section number]	[	271	1

A 8.2.a*
Cure of Flesh
First English edition, first printing, second issue (1934)

Title page: 'A CURE OF FLESH | BY | JAMES GOULD COZZENS | AUTHOR OF "S.S. 'SAN PEDRO' " | LONGMANS, GREEN AND CO. | LONDON • NEW YORK • TORONTO | 1934'.

On copyright page: 'First published . . . . February 1933 | Re-issued in the Longman Novels • August 1934 | Printed in Great Britain'.

Pagination same as first issue.

[A]⁸ (± A1, A2) B–R⁸ S¹⁰

Contents: p. 1: '[gothic] The Longman Novels, 13 | [underline] | [roman] A CURE OF FLESH'; p. 2: ']gothic] The Longman Novels | [underline] | [13 titles beginning with *The Bridge of San Luis Rey* and ending with *A Cure of Flesh]*'; p. 3: title; p. 4: copyright; pp. 5–290: text; pp. 291–292: blank.

Binding: Dark bluish green (#165) V cloth (smooth). Front: '[outlined in dark bluish green on rectangular black panel] A CURE | OF FLESH'. Spine: 'A CURE | OF FLESH | JAMES | GOULD | COZZENS | THE | LONGMAN | NOVELS'.

Dust jacket: Same as first-issue jacket with orange and black triangular label pasted across spine and front, lettered in white: '[on front against orange] THIS | IS | A | [against black] LONGMAN | NOVEL'; '[on spine against black] NET | 3 [slash] 6'.

Publication: The A. M. Heath records indicate that 256 copies were sold and that 412 were remaindered in 1940. 3/6.

Locations: LC; MJB; Princeton (dj).

A 8.2.b
Second English printing: A Cure of Flesh. London, New York & Toronto: Longmans, Green, [1958].

3,050 copies.

A 8.3
Third edition: The Last Adam. Chicago: Readers Library, [1940].

25¢. Wrappers.

A 8.4
Fourth edition: The Last Adam. New York: Editions for the Armed Services, [1944].

#J-285. Wrappers. 95,631 copies.

A 8.5

Fifth edition: A Cure of Flesh. Harmondsworth & New York: Penguin, [1945].

#522. Wrappers. The A. M. Heath records indicate that 84,693 copies a were sold.

A 8.6

Sixth edition: The Last Adam. New York: Harcourt, Brace, 1956.

Harvest #HB-12. $1.25. Wrappers. 9 printings. Reprints noted: 'D.7.59', 'E.10.60', 'F.1.63', 'I.6.69'.

Collation: Substantive variants in the American editions:

Harcourt, Brace (1933)			Harvest Edition (1956; 1969 printing)	
27.20–21	to advance and burn Danbury	[	27.4–5	to escape from burned Danbury
45.9	grasping firmly—	[	45.33–34	grasping the balls firmly—
45.24	Maxwell.	[	46.18	Maxwell?
80.31	effect	[	83.1–2	affect
81.5	effect	[	83.8	affect
93.27	sat	[	96.19	set
100.26	Bros.	[	103.31	Brothers.
101.9	Bros.	[	104.11	Brothers
114.30	ten dollar bills	[	119.2	ten-dollar bills
120.9	ten dollar bills	[	124.23	ten-dollar bills
153.1–2	you'll get yourself into trouble."	[	159.12–13	you'll work yourself up a good hot reinfection."
153.4–5	another	[	159.16	a catheter
165.10	towel	[	172.1	toilet
175.2	women."	[	182.7	women with their legs open."
187.10	"When	[	194.30	"Well
213.30	blame.	[	222.35	blame?
216.7	stealing	[	225.15	steeling
233.29	lightness	[	244.9	lightless
235.1	with chloroform, not morphine	[	245.12–13	with morphine, not chloroform
235.20	unrequired morphine	[	245.34	remaining morphine
243.11	twelve hour shifts	[	254.13	twelve-hour shifts
261.3	could	[	273.8	would

A 9.1.a
First edition, first printing (1934)

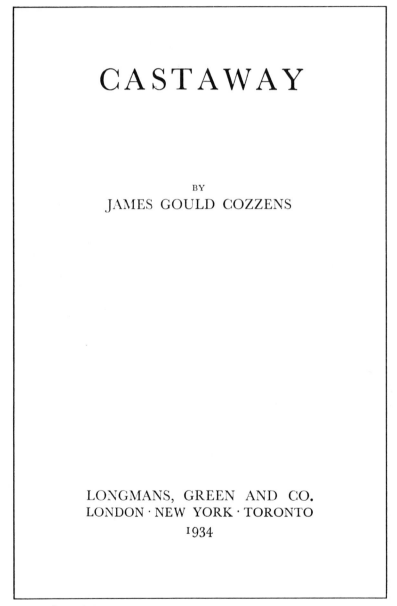

CASTAWAY

BY
JAMES GOULD COZZENS

LONGMANS, GREEN AND CO.
LONDON · NEW YORK · TORONTO
1934

A 9.1.a: 7¾" × 5½"

LONGMANS, GREEN AND CO. LTD.
39 PATERNOSTER ROW, LONDON, E.C.4
6 OLD COURT HOUSE STREET, CALCUTTA
53 NICOL ROAD, BOMBAY
36A MOUNT ROAD, MADRAS

LONGMANS, GREEN AND CO.
114 FIFTH AVENUE, NEW YORK
221 EAST 20TH STREET, CHICAGO
88 TREMONT STREET, BOSTON

LONGMANS, GREEN AND CO.
480 UNIVERSITY AVENUE, TORONTO

Printed in Great Britain

[1–8] 9–181 [182–184]

[A] B–I K–L⁸ M⁴

Contents: pp. 1–2: blank; p. 3: half title; p. 4: *'By the Same Author'* [SSSP and COF]; p. 5: title; p. 6: copyright; p. 7: contents; p. 8: explanatory note; pp. 9–182: text, headed 'I | THE ASCENT INTO THE STORE'; pp. 183–184: blank.

Typography and paper: 4¹⁵⁄₁₆″ (5⅜″) × 3⁵⁄₁₆″. 26 lines per page. Running heads: rectos, chapter titles; versos, 'CASTAWAY'. Laid paper with vertical chain lines.

Binding: Deep purplish pink (#251) V cloth (smooth). Front blindstamped with single-rule frame. Spine goldstamped: '[rule] | *Castaway* | [diamond] | *J. G.* | *Cozzens* | *Longmans* | [rule]'. White wove endpapers. All edges trimmed. Top edge stained deep purplish red (#256).

Dust jacket: Front: yellowish white lettering and line drawing against black; '[slanted rule] | [slanted] CASTAWAY | [slanted rule] | [drawing of man and building, signed 'Isobel R. Beard'] | J. G. COZZENS'. Spine: Yellowish white lettering against black; '[rule] | CASTAWAY | [rule] | J. G. | COZZENS | LONGMANS'. Back quotes reviews for *SSSP* and *COF*. Front flap: blurb for *Castaway*. Back flap blank.

Publication: Unknown number of copies of the first English printing. Published 27 September 1934. 6s. The A. M. Heath records indicate that 763 copies were sold.

Printing: P. 182: 'PRINTED BY WESTERN PRINTING SERVICES LTD., BRISTOL'.

Locations: BL (21 SEP '34); LC; MJB (dj); Princeton (dj).

Proof copy: Book sheets bound in unprinted dark olive brown (#96) wrappers. Leaf A₄ is a cancel. This leaf has the contents on the recto and the explanatory note on the verso; the original leaf was probably cancelled in order to insert the explanatory note on the verso. *Location:* Lilly.

6/- net

CASTAWAY

It is an old conjecture—what would you do and how would you live on a desert island with only a knife, a coconut tree and three yards of string? But, here Mr Cozzens shows the old problem in a new aspect: he leaves one man alone in a vast unoccupied departmental store; unable to leave it but copiously surrounded with food and all the necessities and luxuries of life: a Crusoe surrounded by plenty. It is a fascinating idea—but it was by no means a fascinating adventure; because the very ordinary little man to whom it happened became obsessed with the notion that he was not, after all, alone: that there was an Intruder in those vast spaces, never actually showing himself, but always pursuing, waiting behind corners...

By the Same Author

S. S. "SAN PEDRO"
A TALE OF THE SEA

3s. 6d. net

"Mr Cozzens reminds one vividly of Joseph Conrad. Humour, irony, tragedy, grandeur, are concentrated in this tiny space, and the wings of doom have infinite room to stretch in. The quality of the writing is astonishing."—GERALD GOULD in *The Observer*.

"Told with a minimum of words but with real power and understanding. It certainly grips you ... Mr Cozzens calls his book very simply 'a tale of the sea.' It is a very good tale."—RALPH STRAUS in *The Sunday Times*.

A CURE OF FLESH

3s. 6d. net

"... an exquisite artist ... extraordinarily clear-sighted and just in his view of life."
—SYLVIA LYND in *New Chronicle*.

"A first-class novel ... a technique which is both original and beautiful."—COMPTON MACKENZIE.

"Mr Cozzens is an imaginative realist; and imaginative realism is so rare in fiction that to ascribe it to a novelist is to make very considerable claims on his behalf."—DESMOND MACCARTHY.

Dust jacket for A.9.1.a

CASTAWAY

Alone in a vast Department Store, the sole sur-
vivor of a catastrophe that has destroyed
New York, Mr. Lecky finds himself a com-
monplace little Robinson Crusoe, cut
off from his kind amidst the fan-
tastic plenty of the twentieth century. There is everything to
sustain life in abundance,
and nothing to fear —
except . . . . .

Explanatory note for A9.1.a, p. 8

A 9.2.a
First American edition, first printing (1934)

JAMES GOULD COZZENS

Castaway

RANDOM HOUSE · NEW YORK

1934

A 9.2.a: 7⅜″ × 4¹¹⁄₁₆″

```
          COPYRIGHT,  1 9 3 4 ,

      BY  JAMES  GOULD  COZZENS

  PRINTED  IN  THE  UNITED  STATES  OF  AMERICA
      BY  J.  J.  LITTLE  AND  IVES  COMPANY
                NEW  YORK
        DESIGNED  BY  ROBERT  JOSEPHY
```

[i–iv] v–vi [vii–viii] 9–30 [31–32] 33–49 [50–52] 53–68 [69–70] 71–89 [90–92] 93–113 [114–116] 117–132 [133–134] 135–157 [158–160] 161–171 [172–174] 175–181 [182–184]

[1–10^8 [11]^4 [12]^8

Contents: p. i: half title; p. ii: blank; p. iii: title; p. iv: copyright; pp. v–vi: contents; p. vii: '*1* | *The Ascent into the Store*'; p. viii: blank; pp. 9–181: text, headed with epigraph from *Robinson Crusoe*; pp. 182–184: blank.

Typography and paper: 5¼" (5¹¹⁄₁₆") × 3⅛". 27 lines per page. Running heads: rectos, chapter titles; versos, 'Castaway'. Wove paper.

Binding: Silverstamped black V cloth (smooth). Front: '[script] Castaway'. Spine: '[script] Cast- | away | [roman] JAMES | GOULD | COZZENS | RANDOM | HOUSE'. White wove endpapers. All edges trimmed. Top edge stained greenish blue.

Dust jacket: Printed on tan. Front: '[gray building] | [tapered reddish orange rule] | [gray] CASTAWAY | [tapered reddish orange rule] | [gray] *by* | [reddish orange] JAMES GOULD COZZENS | [gray dot] | [reddish orange] A RANDOM HOUSE BOOK'. Spine: '[vertically] [gray] JAMES GOULD COZZENS [reddish orange] CASTAWAY [gray] RANDOM HOUSE'. Back and flaps printed in gray and reddish orange. Back lists books by 6 Random House authors. Front flap has blurb for *Castaway*. Back flap: ad for The Modern Library.

Publication: Unknown number of copies of the first American printing. Published 7 November 1934. $1.75. The Random House records indicate that 1,410 copies were sold. Copyright #A 78045.

Printing: Printed and bound by J. J. Little & Ives, New York.

Locations: LC (NOV 12 1934); Lilly (dj); MJB (dj).

Collation: Substantive variants between the first English edition and the first American edition:

Longmans, Green (1934)		Random House (1934)
8.1–10	CASTAWAY Alone in a vast Department Store, the sole survivor of a catastrophe that has de- stroyed New York, Mr. Lecky finds himself a com- monplace little Robinson Crusoe, cut off from his kind amidst the fantastic plenty of the twentieth cen- tury. There is everything to	[[omitted]

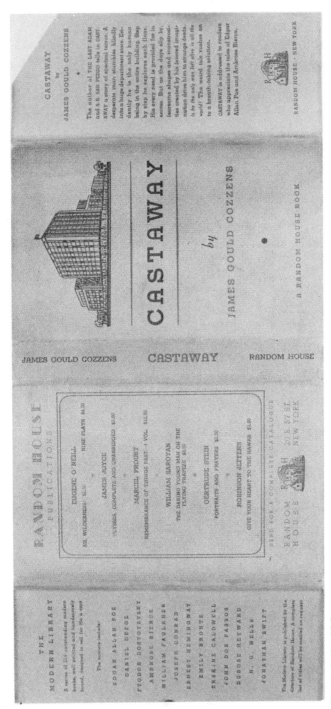

Dust jacket for A 9.2.a

	sustain life in abundance, and nothing to fear—except . . . . .*			
11.13	covered in shining rows with	[	11.5	covered with
11.14	knives.	[	11.6	knives in shining rows.
12.8	distinct	[	11.24	distinctly
18.9–10	Goods and Outing	[	17.9	Goods & Outing
19.1	upon	[	17.25	open
20.1	climb, disquieted, pausing	[	18.22	climb, pausing
20.14	on	[	19.7	in
24.6	exertion	[	22.14	exercise
27.8	on their bowed	[	25.6	on bowed
27.22–23	cascaded in fragments to	[	25.19	fell to fragments at
31.6	Taking	[	28.18	Picking
32.21	found him diagrams	[	30.1	found for him diagrams
33.4–5	with twenty gauge shells	[	30.10	with red shells
48.18	inconscionable	[	45.23	unconscionable
50.15–16	back he was step by step preparing.	[	47.14	back.
50.20	was conveniently close	[	47.17	was close
54.10	removed	[	54.1	moved
61.19–20	face kept coming and going slowly the	[	60.15	face, the
61.21	alone. Hesitating	[	60.16–17	alone kept coming and going slowly. Hesitating
61.22–23	was no longer able to	[	60.19	was unable to
64.3	tap	[	62.18	faucet
64.17–18	shadowed. From the abundance of darkness below, the	[	63.3	shadowed. The
64.19	little. The	[	63.5–6	little of the abundance of darkness below. The
65.12	deep	[	63.21	deeply
67.19	shocked	[	65.22	shook
68.22	satisfied	[	66.18	exhilarated
71.4	light. Up against	[	71.4	light. Against
76.10	beware! His	[	75.16	beware of the wolf! His
76.12	hold	[	75.18	hole
78.3	Burning	[	77.7	Shining
82.8	mind	[	80.27	thought
83.7	a	[	81.23	an
90.18	quiet	[	88.11	quietly
90.22–23	emergency ended for the moment.	[	88.14–15	emergency for the instant ended.
91.3	secure	[	88.21	securely
91.15–16	encounter awaiting his leisure for recognition	[	89.5–6	encounter, waiting on his leisure to be recognised
92.16	helpless	[	93.15	drowsing
92.18	grievous	[	93.17	serious
97.16	ran, howling again	[	97.23	ran, and howled again
97.21	again	[	98.1	once more

*This explanatory note was provided by the English publisher.

97.22	likely, for he	[	98.1	likely. He
98.25	see	[	99.3	reason
99.6	see	[	99.9	recognise
113.20	wracking	[	112.7	racking
113.26	shrieks	[	112.12	outcries
118.8–9	More fundamentally	[	118.21–22	Fundamentally
119.3	improvement	[	119.13	benefit
119.4	would make in his	[	119.14	would be to his
119.18	This had taken little time, but	[	119.27	This took only a little while, but
121.24	bins full	[	121.23	binfuls
126.22	one	[	126.8	he
128.4	neglected stubble	[	127.11	neglected first stubble
128.21	suit at random. Removing	[	127.26	suit. Removing
128.24	suit	[	128.2	coat
128.25	coat	[	128.3	one
130.10–11	cloth better, he	[	129.11	cloth, he
134.3–4	fainter, as though it did indeed proceed	[	132.20–21	fainter; it must, indeed, proceed
136.12	cook some.	[	136.1	cook.
137.1	Prising	[	136.14	Prying
138.14	orchid	[	137.25	violet
139.13	mass	[	138.20	mess
140.23	soup-stock	[	139.25	vegetables
142.25	remembrance	[	141.19–20	membrane
152.3	taps	[	149.22	faucets
157.25	for	[	154.25	since
158.17	for such fancy	[	155.14	for fancy
161.6	so certainly needed	[	157.20	so needed
163.9	misuse	[	161.27	disuse
163.11	words	[	162.1	crowds
168.18	systole	[	166.15	beat
168.22–23	little, dissipating	[	166.19–20	little, becoming dissipated
169.2	reminded	[	166.24	reminding
170.18	fear	[	168.9	freer
171.10	two	[	168.26	too
174.14– 175.11	outdoors. Rain in its desolation would be pouring down all over the city, augmenting the catastrophe. That catastrophe it was, Mr. Lecky had never doubted, though he had wondered so little. It was pressed in with his misery now, made immediate and overwhelming. He might suppose he had lived, like those fish he had tried to feed and the birds in their cages downstairs, a little	[	175.12–13	outdoors. [paragraph] Mr. Lecky

longer than the world.
[paragraph] Mr. Lecky had
not only the sense of ca-
tastrophe, but—holding his
head to see better—all the
proof he needed of it. How
otherwise came so great a
wealth of things, materials,
to be untended? Only one
concern could be greater
than riches; it must be
death. Six days? Who alive
could wait a day to claim
and defend so much of
value? Granted then, a
dead world. Mr. Lecky

175.11–13	motionless, for more than the thought of universal disaster, the misery	[	175.13	motionless; the misery
180.9	illuminating	[	179.21	illuminated
181.6	now learned	[	180.15	now found out

A 9.3
Third edition: New York: Editions for the Armed Services, [1945].

#S-4. Wrappers. 141,268 copies

A 9.4
Fourth edition: New York: Bantam, [1952].

#1007. 25¢. Wrappers.

A 9.5
Fifth edition: London: Transworld, [1952].

Corgi #1007. 2s. Wrappers.

A 9.6.a and A 9.6.b
Sixth edition: S.S. San Pedro and Castaway. See A 7.6.a and A 7.6.b.

A 9.7.a
Seventh edition, first printing: New York: Harcourt, Brace & World, [1967].

"Uniform Edition." $3.50.

Collation: Substantive variants in the American editions:

Random House (1934)			Harcourt, Brace & World "Uniform Edition" (1967)	
9	[epigraph at head of text]	[	vi	[epigraph on separate page]
36.12	on	[	21.29	in
58.4–5	[space break]	[	36.6–7	[no space break]
59.25	and squeak	[	37.16–17	and a squeak
65.21–22	leaped and shook, showed	[	41.26	leaped, and showed

71.20	nor	[	44.15	or
118.13	disturbed, and	[	75.19	disturbed to act, and
151.4–5	time, and as it was to hap- pen, for the last time of his own will and walking like a free man, Mr. Lecky	[	98.3	time, Mr. Lecky

A 9.7.b
Seventh edition, Harvest printing: New York: Harcourt, Brace & World, [1968].

Harvest #HB 134. $1.15. Wrappers.

A 9.8
Eighth edition: [London]: Longmans, [1968].

The A. M. Heath records indicate that 2,135 copies were sold.

A 10 MEN AND BRETHREN

A 10.1.a
First edition, first printing [1936]

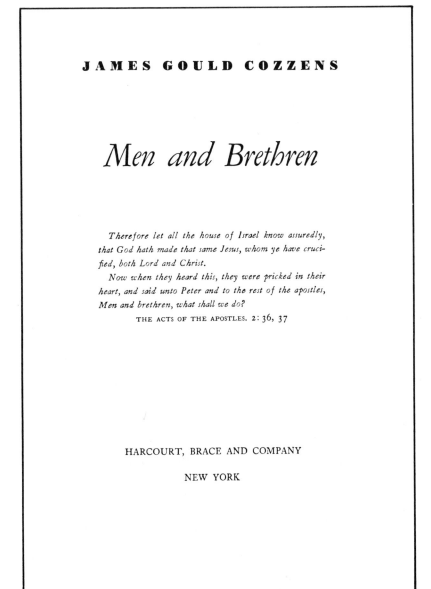

JAMES GOULD COZZENS

Men and Brethren

Therefore let all the house of Israel know assuredly,
that God hath made that same Jesus, whom ye have cruci-
fied, both Lord and Christ.
Now when they heard this, they were pricked in their
heart, and said unto Peter and to the rest of the apostles,
Men and brethren, what shall we do?

THE ACTS OF THE APOSTLES. 2: 36, 37

HARCOURT, BRACE AND COMPANY

NEW YORK

A 10.1.a: 7^{15}⁄₁₆″ × 5¼″

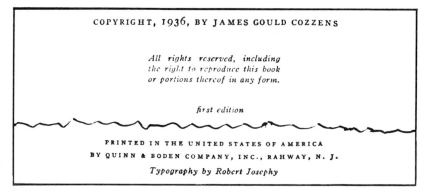

[i–iv] [1–2] 3–282 [283–284]

[1–18]⁸

Contents: p. i: half title; p. ii: 'by the same author | S.S. SAN PEDRO | THE LAST ADAM'; p. iii: title; p. iv: copyright; p. 1: half title; p. 2: blank; pp. 3–282: text, headed 'One'; pp. 283–284: blank.

Typography and paper: 5½″ (5¾″) × 3½″. 25 lines per page. Running heads: rectos and versos, 'MEN AND BRETHREN'. Wove paper.

Binding: Goldstamped varnished black V cloth (smooth). Spine: 'COZZENS | *Men and* | *Brethren* | HARCOURT, BRACE | AND COMPANY'. Cream wove endpapers. All edges trimmed. Top edge stained reddish brown.

Dust jacket: Front: '[white lettering on dark blue panel] MEN | AND | BRETHREN | [painting of city street, signed 'J. O'H. COSGRAVE II'] | [white lettering on black panel] by | JAMES GOULD COZZENS | author of The Last Adam'. Spine: '[white lettering on dark blue panel] MEN | AND | BRETHREN | JAMES | GOULD | COZZENS | [oval painting of church on white panel] | [white lettering on dark blue panel] HARCOURT, BRACE | AND COMPANY'. Back and flaps printed in blue. Back: blurbs for *LA* and *SSSP*. Front flap: blurb for *M&B*. Back flap: excerpt from *Time* review of *LA* and biographical note on Cozzens; replaced in later printings by "*First reviews of* | MEN AND BRETHREN'.

Publication: 10,000 copies of the first printing. Published 2 January 1936. $2.50. Copyright #A 91197. The Brandt & Brandt records indicate that 9,011 copies were sold through 1938, also that 314 copies were sold to Blue Ribbon Books in 1937.

Printing: Printed and bound by Quinn & Boden, Rahway, N.J.

Locations: BL (10 FEB '36); LC (JAN 15 1936); Lilly (dj); MJB (dj); PSt.

Review copy: Free front endpaper stamped in dark blue: 'REVIEW COPY | PUBLICATION DATE | JAN 2 1935 PRICE $ 2.50'. *Location:* MJB.

A 10.1.b
Second printing: New York: Harcourt, Brace, [1936].

On copyright page: 'Second printing, January, 1936'.

Dust jacket for A10.1.a

A 10.1.c
Third printing: New York: Harcourt, Brace, [1958].

On copyright page: 'C.11.57'.

$4.00.

A 10.2.a
First English edition, first printing (1936)

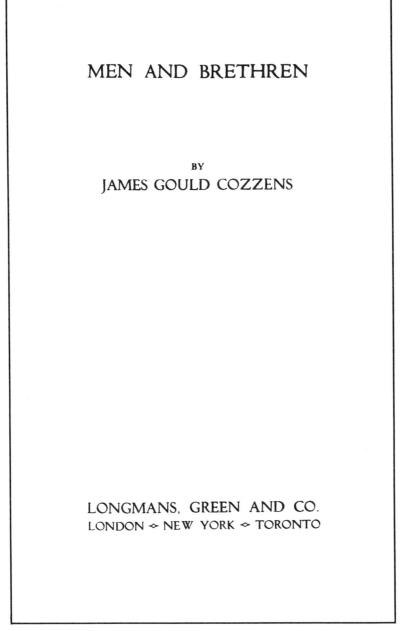

MEN AND BRETHREN

BY

JAMES GOULD COZZENS

LONGMANS, GREEN AND CO.
LONDON ◇ NEW YORK ◇ TORONTO

A 10.2.a: 7⅜″ × 4¹⁵⁄₁₆″

[1–8] 9–309 [310–312]

[A]⁴ B–I K–U⁸

Contents: p. 1: blank; p. 2: *'By the Same Author' [SSSP, COF, Castaway]*; p. 3: half title; p. 4: blank; p. 5: title; p. 6: copyright; p. 7: contents; p. 8: blank; pp. 9–309: text, headed 'PART I'; p. 310: 'PRINTED BY | WESTERN PRINTING SERVICES LTD., BRISTOL'; pp. 311–312: blank.

Typography and paper: 5⅛" (5½") × 3⁵⁄₁₆". 25 lines per page. Running heads: rectos and versos, 'MEN AND BRETHREN'. Wove paper.

Binding: Strong reddish orange (#35) V cloth (smooth). Spine stamped in dark blue: 'MEN AND | BRETHREN | [decoration] | J. G. | COZZENS | Longmans'. Cream wove endpapers. Top and fore-edges trimmed. Bottom edge rough-trimmed.

Dust jacket: Printed on off-white. Front: 'men | and | [drawing of 7 heads in black, orange, and blue, signed 'J. Z. Arkinson'] | brethren | J.G. COZZENS'. Spine: 'men | and | breth- | ren | [3 heads in black, orange, and blue] | J.G. | COZZENS | LONGMANS'. Back: blurbs for *Castaway, SSSP,* and *COF.* Front flap: blurb for *M&B.* Back flap: announcement for *Longmans' Log.*

Publication: Unknown number of copies of the first printing. Published 8 March 1936. 7/6. The A. M. Heath records indicate that 736 copies were sold and that 588 were remaindered in 1940, but the Brandt & Brandt records indicate that 4,132 copies were sold.

Printing: Printed by Western Printing Services Ltd., Bristol.

Locations: BL (21 FEB '36); MJB (dj).

Collation: Substantive variants between the first American edition and the first English edition:

Harcourt, Brace (1936)		Longmans, Green (1936)	
iii	[6-line epigraph]	[5	[epigraph omitted]
3.1–2	impatient peal, while	[9.1–2	impatient, while

men and brethren

J.G. COZZENS

LONGMANS

"I don't think," wrote the first critic of this story, "that I have ever read a book which portrays as convincingly the hysterical and feverish rush of life in a great city to-day. Ernest Cudlipp, the parson, is a most truthful and likeable portrait. He is a giver, and he glories in his ability to handle other people's affairs. Cocksure, coping perpetually with at least two affairs at once, argumentative and absurdly kind. Ernest is a very real person and one follows him through one day of his much harassed life, convinced that he is doing what he believes to be right, even when ..."

"I agree entirely," wrote the second reader. "I read the book with real excitement."

Other Novels by
JAMES GOULD COZZENS
described
on the back of this cover

7/6 net

By The Same Author

CASTAWAY
6s. net

"Unusual and brilliant novel ... this really is a brilliant piece of work ... a triumph of imaginative realism."—A. J. Cronin.

"A study of terror and madness ... the madness of a creature cut off from its kind and driven, by the nightmare of solitude to self-destruction. A brilliant and truly terrifying essay."—London Mercury.

SS. "SAN PEDRO"
3s 6d net

"Mr Cozzens reminds one vividly of Joseph Conrad; but one feels that he would have written his book just as he has written it even if Joseph Conrad had never existed. ... Humour, irony, tragedy, grandeur, are contained in this tiny space, and the wings of Cozzens have infinite room to stretch in. The quality of the writing is astonishing—Gerald Gould.

A CURE OF FLESH
3s. 6d. net

"... an exquisite artist ... extraordinarily clear-sighted and just in his view of life."—Sylvia Lynd.

"Mr Cozzens is an imaginative realist; and imaginative realism is so rare in fiction that to ascribe it to a novelist is to make very considerable claims on his behalf."—Desmond MacCarthy.

LONGMANS' LOG is issued periodically. It tells you all about Longmans' BOOKS AND AUTHORS and will be sent FREE on APPLICATION.

Printed in Great Britain

Dust jacket for A 10.2.a

4.4–6	left. The Senior Warden, at some sacrifice of his personal convenience, almost always got in Fridays— even as hot a Friday as this. Told	[	10.4	left. Told
6.22	books. [no paragraph] At	[	12.25– 13.1	books. [paragraph] At
11.5	shirt	[	17.18	vest
11.14	left and right	[	18.2	left to right
17.3–4	how." [paragraph] Once	[	24.2	how." [no paragraph] Once
21.17	when, but	[	28.23–24	when it was, but
23.1	reminding	[	30.9	telling
23.25– 24.1	For a couple of years now	[	31.13	For some time now
26.3	job	[	33.22	business
30.9	He's twenty-two	[	38.12	He's about twenty-two
30.18–19	name. It was called *Sun Poems*. Somebody	[	38.23	name. Somebody
33.14	tasted it,	[	41.22	tasted,
33.14–15	Johannisberger	[	41.22	Johannesberger
34.1	some	[	42.10	an
39.6	to say that	[	48.1	to tell him that
39.22	something	[	48.18	it
44.16	of	[	53.16	on
47.15–16	swung back. Unable	[	56.25– 57.1	swung in; and, unable
48.6	creatures	[	57.19	creature
50.4	vial	[	59.21	phial
51.2	these	[	60.21	those
52.14	people benefit	[	62.11	people the benefit
56.20	woman's	[	67.3	women's
59.25	how	[	70.15	why
59.25	out from under?"	[	70.15	out?"
61.9	vial	[	72.2	phial
65.9	position where you can only choose	[	76.8–9	position which makes you choose
65.18–19	her. [paragraph] When	[	76.18	her. [no paragraph] When
67.1	Ernest	[	77.24	he
67.3	he	[	78.2	Ernest
70.17–18	Elizabethan. Back in 1929 they had changed it to	[	81.24–25	Elizabethan for 1929. It was changed then to
72.10	For	[	83.19	To
74.12	any	[	85.25	a
74.14	as	[	86.2	being
74.18	life. His	[	86.7	life, for his
74.19	assuredly	[	86.8	undoubtedly
74.24	there	[	86.14	these
78.16	Hello	[	90.9	Hollo
83.15–16	business. [no paragraph] Flushing	[	95.19–20	business. [paragraph] Flushing

84.6–7	implied. [paragraph] "All	[	96.11–12	implied. [no paragraph] "All
84.11–12	Wilber, affronted, would	[	96.17–18	Wilber would
88.2–3	ice—" [paragraph] He pushed the door open with	[	100.15–24	ice——" [paragraph] Unable to keep down his laughter, he nonetheless called sharply, "Lily, if you're too lazy to walk as far as the corner, I don't think you deserve any ice cream." [paragraph] There was a mute alarmed pause in the lower darkness and Lily quavered finally, "I thought you might want me, Mr. Cudlipp, so I better not go out. They'll send it up." [paragraph] Ernest pushed the door with
92.22	further	[	106.10	farther
93.17	in the process	[	107.8	in fact
109.20	quibbles	[	124.18	squibbles
109.21	Ingersoll	[	124.19	Ingersol
110.16	astrophysics	[	125.17	asterophysics
111.11	a	[	126.12	an
113.2	predominately	[	128.6	predominantly
115.9	Jesus	[	130.18	Jesu
128.24	shaky	[	145.3	grimy
133.3–4	brought. I	[	149.17	brought up. I
136.8	Ernest. [no paragraph] "That's	[	152.23–24	Ernest. [paragraph] "That's
156.7	sounded	[	174.9	came
163.11	jauntiness, the	[	181.25–182.1	jauntiness, almost, the
164.13–14	It wasn't hard, it wasn't pleasant, to	[	183.3–4	It was neither hard nor pleasant to
166.10	took you two	[	185.3	took two
168.7	write too	[	187.3	write to too
172.8	in the blaze	[	191.10	in blaze
180.1	proselyting	[	199.21–22	proselytizing
181.1	calls him when	[	201.2	calls when
186.17	Hawleys'	[	206.24	Hawley's
187.1	as	[	207.9	was
188.2	hepatitis	[	208.13	hepatis
189.18	wish	[	210.8	like
190.8	at	[	210.23	to
194.3–4	bed wanted no name	[	215.2	bed was beyond name
195.7–8	aimlessly	[	216.10	aimless
203.21–22	distracted while he met the dreadful, unanswerable question. What	[	225.14–15	distracted, guess the dreadful unanswerable question, What
205.11	people's	[	227.8	peoples'

209.17–18	on one of the methods. It	[	231.18–19	on the method of Saint Sul-pice. It
216.24	better eat with	[	239.15	better have lunch with
227.20	angus dei	[	251.9	*agnus dei*
228.21–22	morning. We'll	[	252.13	morning. Come. We'll
229.11	to. Yet	[	253.2–3	to. What's—Yet
231.12–13	farther." [paragraph] He	[	255.10	farther." [no paragraph] He
231.22	Alice	[	255.20	she
232.6	seventy dollars	[	256.6	seventy-some dollars
232.25	ears, curls	[	257.2	ears wisps and curls
234.6	purpose. Having	[	258.9–10	purpose, and having
234.10–11	years and you're bound to miss him; just as a	[	258.14–16	years. That's the most im-portant thing. Perhaps you didn't like it all, but a
234.13	insufferable	[	258.18	unendurable
235.19	heat. In the fall	[	260.2	heat. By fall
236.17	the	[	261.3	a
237.6	answered	[	261.19	said
238.10–11	*evil* . . . [paragraph] Now	[	262.22	*evil.* . . . [no paragraph] Now
241.2–3	sentence." [paragraph] You	[	265.15–16	sentence." [no paragraph] You
243.24	ruthlessly." [no paragraph] On	[	268.16–17	ruthlessly." [paragraph] On
243.25	Kalender	[	268.17	Calendar
245.7	Διὰ δὲ τὰς πορνείας—	[	270.1	Λὶα δὲ τας πορνίας——
249.16	heart. Perhaps it was like	[	274.15	heart, which must be much like
250.9–11	trifle—it was Jeremy Tay-lor's wild, indeterminate, infinite appetite of man—the	[	275.10	trifle the
254.17	Benham	[	280.4	Winkler
262.5	the	[	288.10	as a
263.23–24	O.H.T.!" That amused him. He did not want to think of any other aspect of it at the moment. Sitting	[	290.5	O.H.T." Sitting
269.16	must contain some	[	296.2–3	must have been some
273.14	had told her who	[	300.3–4	had said who
280.5	dignity	[	307.8	importance

A 10.2.b
Second English printing: London, New York & Toronto: Longmans, Green, [1948].

On copyright page: 'Reprinted by Novographic Process 1948'.

6s. The A. M. Heath records indicate that 824 copies were sold and that 4,094 were remaindered in 1952.

A 10.2.c
Third English printing: London, New York & Toronto: Longmans, Green, [1958].

On copyright page: '*Issued in this edition 1958*'.

16s. 5,050 copies printed. The A. M. Heath records indicate that 2,686 copies were sold.

A 10.3
Third edition: New York: Harcourt Brace Jovanovich, [1970].
"Uniform Edition." $5.95.

Collation: Substantive variants in the American editions:

Harcourt, Brace (1936)			Harcourt Brace Jovanovich "Uniform Edition" (1970)	
3.1–2	Ernest let the telephone ring, peal on impatient peal, while	[	3.1–2	The telephone was ringing. Ernest let the ringing go on while
3.2–3	cigarette. He thrust it	[	3.3–4	cigarette. Taking one from the package he found, he put it
9.10	able to preach	[	7.14–15	able to resume preaching
16.17–18	peace—turning down the avenue he was given a last glimpse. The	[	12.2–3	peace. Now going south on the avenue he got a last glimpse—the
16.19	behind; on	[	12.4	behind the church, and on
19.9–11	productions. [paragraph] Bad on the stage, off it Alice was even worse. She	[	13.27–29	productions. [paragraph] If on the stage there was little to recommend Alice, off it there was even less. She
20.23–21.1	rightness. Alice wasn't real; she wasn't at all what she struggled so unconvincingly to appear. [paragraph] The	[	14.27–30	rightness. The Alice she tried to palm off on you was bogus, not at all the actual Alice. [paragraph] The
21.24	really	[	15.17	almost
23.25	Rome respectable. For	[	16.28	Rome socially acceptable here. For
28.17	nodded	[	19.31	said
31.24	it," urged Ernest.	[	22.3	it," Ernest said.
32.9	Oh, Lord! You	[	22.11	Oh, I forgot! You
33.25	was so obviously an	[	23.14	was unmistakably an
34.4	impatiently	[	23.19	impatient
35.12–13	and are really able to. You're	[	24.15–16	and find you can. You're
37.3	admitted	[	25.17	said
39.4	with all viciousness at	[	26.27–28	with happy malevolence at
40.6–7	know," he corrected her indulgently. "Compassion	[	27.18	know. Compassion
43.1	amiable common sense, rather	[	29.8	amiable receptiveness, rather
43.9–10	and for a fractional second, disengaged, still	[	29.16–17	and, for the time of a moment, disengaged, held still
43.12–13	nothing. Like coolness in	[	29.18–20	nothing. He could measure

	the night, he could measure the inflow of physical refreshment and			the inflow of physical refreshment like coolness in the night and
45.10	desperate	[	30.28	stern
45.11	dreary	[	30.49	flaccid
47.10–11	acquaintanceship entirely artificial. Her	[	32.9–10	acquaintanceship altogether nominal. Her
47.19	being cheap and silly, it	[	32.17	being vulgar and nasty, it
47.26–48.1	laughed. "I don't know why. It certainly isn't the	[	32.24–25	laughed. "What you'd do, I mean. Not the
55.12	granting	[	37.22	provided
56.4	responsibility	[	38.2–3	capability
56.10–11	seen—her background and training were inevitable and obvious—her	[	38.7–8	seen—facts of her background and training spoke through her—her
56.15	home very likely ugly and tasteless	[	38.13	home perhaps architecturally tasteless
58.2	slapped	[	39.11	rubbed
58.2–3	head lightly. "Lord	[	39.11	head. "Lord
58.3	sighed	[	39.12	said
66.10	Take	[	44.20	Swallow
70.18–20	in 1929 they had changed it to make Job conform to the Roman Vulgate. [paragraph] He	[	47.13–16	in 1901 they rephrased it. That reconstituted flesh of Job's had been just destroyed, no agency specified. [paragraph] He
72.10	marvels	[	48.17	vagaries
73.22	fool	[	49.16	simple
74.14–15	needing	[	49.31	requiring
82.21	agreed	[	55.9	said
83.14–15	Action. However, he	[	55.25–26	Action. At the same time he
83.15	getting deep in the	[	55.26	getting into the
83.22	be got at any	[	55.32–33	be reached any
84.22	requirement	[	56.22	qualification
92.24	far-from-distinguished	[	61.31–32	far-from-consequential
93.2	dangerously	[	61.34	frigidly
93.2–3	fact greatly restrained. By nature he was courteous	[	62.1–2	fact controlled and tempered by a nature courteous
93.25	remarkable	[	62.21	admirable
99.11–12	either. That part of it is really	[	66.11	either. A state of affairs really
101.19	sighed	[	67.27	paused
112.6	want	[	74.18	like
113.2–3	congregation. It was. Carl	[	75.4	congregation. They found it so. Carl
114.11	Pharisees	[	76.1	pew holders
121.5–7	settled." [paragraph] "In that sense, it is settled already," Ernest objected. "You'll	[	80.13–14	settled." [paragraph] Ernest said, "You'll

121.11	Wilber echoed him. He	[	80.18	Wilber said. He
121.18	inquired	[	80.24	said
129.23	nor	[	85.34	or
131.15	nor	[	87.2	or
136.17–18	Cudlipp? I hope that's going to work out. I	[	90.10–11	Cudlipp? Is too much being asked of him? I
137.9–10	Your point was good. . . ."	[	90.25	You had a nice point. . . ."
145.12	nor	[	96.2	or
161.2–4	tiptoe from the room. [paragraph] "Good," Ernest nodded to him. [paragraph] Alice	[	106.7–10	tiptoe toward the door. [paragraph] "Do," Ernest said. [paragraph] Alice
163.1–2	Ernest. "Egg me on	[	107.21–22	Ernest. "Get me started on
176.4	typewrite	[	116.5	type
179.6–7	soon lost any consciousness of being officers	[	118.6–7	soon stopped seeing themselves as officers
181.6	admitted	[	119.18	said
208.8	nor	[	136.32	or
208.8	nor	[	136.33	or
237.14–15	house had that dull, horrible melancholy of an enforced idleness; a helpless	[	156.10–11	house with melancholy of ennui, of helpless

A 11 ASK ME TOMORROW

A 11.1.a
First edition, first printing [1940]

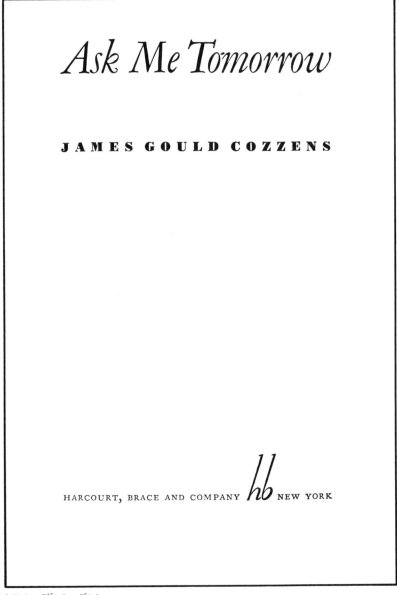

Ask Me Tomorrow

JAMES GOULD COZZENS

HARCOURT, BRACE AND COMPANY *hb* NEW YORK

A 11.1.a: 7^{15}⁄₁₆″ × 5^{5}⁄₁₆″

[i–vi] [1–2] 3–338

[1–21]⁸ [22]⁴

Contents: p. i: half title; p. ii: *'Other books by James Gould Cozzens' [SSSP, LA, M&B];* p. iii: title; p. iv: copyright; p. v: 4 lines from *Troilus and Cressida;* p. vi: blank; p. 1: half title; p. 2: blank; pp. 3–338: text, headed *'One'*.

Typography and paper: 5¾″ (6³⁄₁₆″) × 3⅝″. 32 lines per page. Running heads: rectos and versos, 'ASK ME TOMORROW'. Wove paper.

Binding: Medium reddish brown (#43) buckram. Spine silverstamped: 'COZZENS | *Ask Me* | *Tomorrow* | HARCOURT, BRACE | AND COMPANY'. Cream-colored end-papers. All edges trimmed. Top edge stained reddish brown.

Dust jacket: Front and spine have light reddish barown and white net pattern. Front: '[black] Ask Me | Tomorrow | A NEW NOVEL BY | [on black and light brown panel in blue outlined in brown]JAMES | GOULD | COZZENS'. Spine: '[5 lines on black and light brown panel] [gray outlined in light brown]Ask Me | Tomorrow | [white outlined in light brown] JAMES | GOULD | COZZENS | [below panel in black] HARCOURT, BRACE | AND COMPANY'. Back: photo of Cozzens and biographical note. front flap: blurb for *AMT*. Back flap: 5 comments on Cozzens from reviews.

Publication: 6,500 copies of the first printing. Published 13 June 1940. $2.50. Copyright #A 141885.

Printing: Printed and bound by Quinn & Boden, Rahway, N.J.

Locations: LC (JUN 19 1940); MJB (dj).

Review copy: Stamped on free front endpaper in dark gray: 'REVIEW COPY | PUBLICATION DATE | JUN 13 1940 PRICE $2.50'. *Location:* MJB.

A 11.1.b
Harbrace Modern Classics printings: New York: Harcourt, Brace, [1952].

3 printings. Reprint noted: 'B.10.57'.

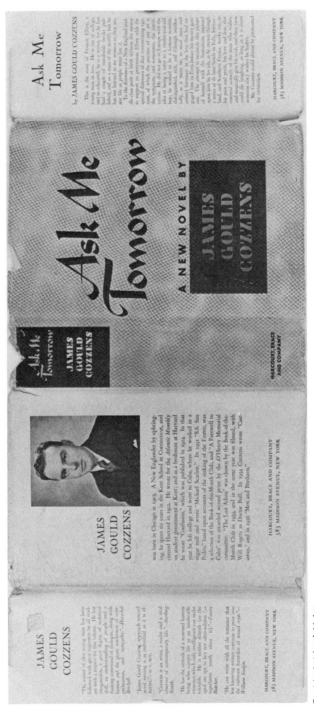

Dust jacket for A11.1.a

A 11.2.a
First English edition, first printing [1940]

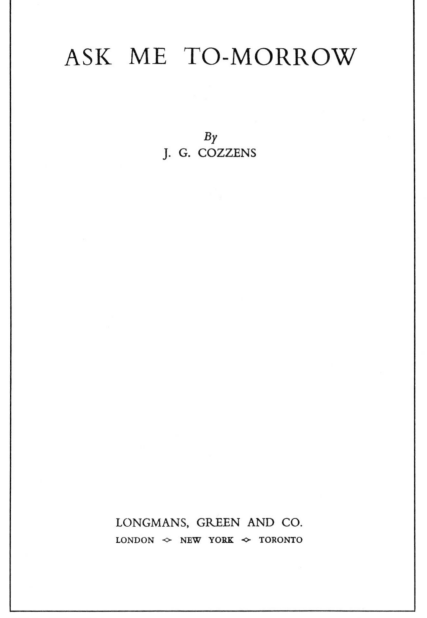

ASK ME TO-MORROW

By
J. G. COZZENS

LONGMANS, GREEN AND CO.
LONDON ◇ NEW YORK ◇ TORONTO

A 11.2.a: 7¼″ × 4¹³⁄₁₆″

LONGMANS, GREEN AND CO. LTD.

39 PATERNOSTER ROW, LONDON, E.C.4.
17 CHITTARANJAN AVENUE, CALCUTTA
NICOL ROAD, BOMBAY
36A MOUNT ROAD, MADRAS

LONGMANS, GREEN AND CO.

55 FIFTH AVENUE, NEW YORK
221 EAST 20TH STREET, CHICAGO
88 TREMONT STREET, BOSTON

LONGMANS, GREEN AND CO.

215 VICTORIA STREET, TORONTO

First published 1940

PRINTED IN GREAT BRITAIN
BY WESTERN PRINTING SERVICES LTD., BRISTOL

[1–8] 9–318 [319–320]

[A] B–I K–U⁸

Contents: pp. 1–2: blank; p. 3: half title; p. 4: 'OTHER BOOKS BY J. G. COZZENS' *[SOP, SSSP, COF, Castaway, M&B]*; p. 5: title; p. 6: copyright; p. 7: epigraph; p. 8: blank; pp. 9–318: text, headed 'CHAPTER I | I'; pp. 319–320: blank.

Typography and paper: 5½" (5¹³⁄₁₆") × 3½". 33 lines per page. Running heads: rectos and versos, 'ASK ME TO-MORROW'. Wove paper.

Binding: Medium violet (#211) V cloth (smooth). Front: 'ASK ME TO = MORROW | J. G. Cozzens'. Spine: 'ASK | ME | TO- | MORROW | J. G. | COZZENS | LONGMANS'. White wove endpapers. All edges trimmed.

Dust jacket: Front: '[light yellow slanted script on reddish brown] 'Ask me | to-morrow | [star] | James Gould Cozzens'. Spine: '[reddish brown on greenish yellow] ASK ME | TO= | MORROW | [star] | J. G. | COZZENS | [ship device] | LONGMANS'. Back: ads for 4 Longmans books printed in reddish brown on greenish yellow. Front flap: blurb for *AMT* and price. Back flap: *'Printed in Great Britain* [colophon]'.

Publication: Unknown number of copies of the first English printing. Published 7 October 1940. 8/6. The A. M. Heath records indicate that 596 copies were sold, but the Brandt & Brandt records state that 2,742 copies were sold. A 1942 Longmans "Cheap Edition" at 4/6 sold 892 copies. Not seen. This "Cheap Edition" was probably a new binding of the first-printing sheets.

Printing: See copyright page.

Locations: BL (3 OCT 40); Harcourt Brace Jovanovich (dj); MJB.

Collation: Substantive variants between the first American edition and the first English edition:

Harcourt, Brace (1940)		Longmans, Green (1940)	
21.9–10	distraught accessories-be-fore-the-fact to	[25.32–33	distraught principals in the second degree to
23.8	twisted	[27.27	took
23.18–19	her. [paragraph] She	[28.3	her. [no paragraph] She
39.10	clear	[42.18	clearer

8/6 NET

Readers of 'S.S. SAN PEDRO' will have no doubts about the quality of Mr. Cozzens's writing. Here, he presents a full-length modern novel, which is primarily a character-study of a pleasant but egoistical young American in Europe. Francis Ellery has had a minor success as a novelist but has made no money; so he takes a post as a tutor to the lively but half-invalided son of a wealthy American globe-trotter, and is henceforth torn between rival interests —his next book, his job, the girl he really loves, other maidens who attract him, and above all himself. He is candid enough to confess to himself that he has 'a marked taste for wine and women.' He is honourable enough not to let his duty be entirely outplaced by his desires—but only just.

ASK ME TO-MORROW
*
J. G. COZZENS

Ask me to-morrow

★

James Gould Cozzens

LONGMANS

Stella Gibbons
CHRISTMAS AT
COLD COMFORT FARM
AND OTHER STORIES

There are sixteen stories here, most of them cheerful and they are about all kinds of people. The title story should give great pleasure to all those who have asked repeatedly for "more about Cold Comfort Farm".

Desmond Hawkins
LIGHTER THAN DAY

The story of two brothers who grew up in the ominous lull between the last war and the present one, and are in revolt against the complacency of the world into which they were born.

Josephine Bell
ALL IS VANITY

This book marks the return of Josephine Bell to detection, and the reappearance of that attractive pair, the Wintringhams. As in all her books the mystery and the writing are excellent and the people are very real.

John Dollond
A GENTLEMAN HANGS

A detective story of the new school with good characterization and witty dialogue. The detection too is good, and the solution of the bizarre mystery comes as a real surprise.

ENGLAND

Printed in Great Britain

Dust jacket for A 11.2.a

60.3	O.K.,	[	62.21	Oh,
60.31	end, still	[	63.16	end. Still
61.15–16	skis." He did not. He	[	63.31–64.3	skis." He had not said it. His feeling about Walter's misfortune was too complicated. Trying to ignore it, he had been anxious to pretend that it did not exist. He was unwilling to refer to it. Sympathetically, he did not want to show that he ever noticed it; but his sympathy was mixed with other feelings. He
62.15–16	instead?	[	64.33	instead.
72.24	good a joke	[	74.11	exhilarating a jest
73.21	motormen's	[	75.6	motorman's
79.10	ten-thousand	[	80.14	ten thousand
82.12	Christiania	[	83.5	stem
82.32	pole	[	83.25	stick
83.19	pole	[	84.10	stick
83.21	pole	[	84.12	stick
83.29	pole	[	84.19	stick
103.14	a	[	102.11	an
111.31–112.1	said. [paragraph] Maggie	[	110.6–7	said. [no paragraph] Maggie
123.24	*VIEW	[	121.14	VIEW
126.19	while	[	124.3	and
126.30	Wellesley. With	[	124.12–15	Wellesley. He remembered her crinkly blonde hair, the faintly husky tone of her voice, the tone of her skin, dusty, faintly freckled, about the same gold tone as her hair. With
157.32	a	[	152.215	an
161.7	Aw	[	155.13	Ah
165.6	late	[	165.5	later
172.2–3	dead. [paragraph] Francis	[	165.20	dead. [no paragraph] Francis
177.29	its	[	171.1	the
183.24	fine	[	176.13	grand
183.32	curb	[	176.20	kerb
186.10	monster.	[	178.9	monster,
188.23	shirt	[	180.16	skirt
189.1	life-sized	[	180.25	life-size
216.17–18	lessons ordinarily took	[	206.11	lessons took
224.24	his other arm,	[	213.27	his arm
240.29	abandon	[	228.16	abandoned
240.29	strike	[	228.17	struck
241.2	put	[	228.20	set

245.6	Itsy-bitsy	[	232.12	Itsy-bits
249.15	circumstance	[	236.7	circumstances
249.31	permit	[	236.23	permis
252.10–11	hard. [paragraph] "You're	[	238.30	hard. [no paragraph] "You're
258.5	curb	[	244.9	kerb
258.10	obscurity	[	244.14	gloom
258.14	way.	[	244.18	way!
269.1	of	[	254.7	to
270.23	of	[	255.29	off
274.21–22	own. [paragraph] "Here	[	259.17–18	own. [no paragraph] "Here
274.24–25	lips. [paragraph] "And	[	259.19	lips. [no paragraph] "And
275.1	of	[	259.29	to
275.2	of	[	259.30	to
288.19–20	move. [paragraph] "Walter!	[	272.16–17	move. [no paragraph] "Walter!
305.19	knew	[	288.5	know
307.20	poles	[	290.3	sticks
310.1	pole	[	292.5	stick
311.32	direction	[	294.1	directions
313.30	shift	[	295.28	shaft
314.32	peddling	[	296.27–28	pedalling
319.5	on	[	300.20	in
325.22	whose	[	306.18	in his
325.23	whose	[	306.19	his
325.24	had been so	[	306.20	so
330.16–17	It will be	[	310.32	It's going to be
332.1	of course	[	312.13	no doubt
332.7	come, admire,	[	312.19	come, see, admire,
332.15–16	had gone too	[	312.27–28	had begun to go too
332.19–20	which upset everything.	[	312.31–32	which staggered and smashed things.
333.6	lark.	[	313.16–18	lark. Gwen might allow that love laughed at locksmiths; but at common sense love would laugh over Gwen's dead body.
335.12–13	lounge. [paragraph] "If	[	315.16	lounge. [no paragraph] "If
337.17	Well, it is so hard to tell. I	[	317.21	Well, I
337.18–23	faltered; but he was, he remembered, always fortunate. When he wished, the wish came true. When he did not know what on earth to do, Mrs. Cunningham, all unaware, told him; and all unasked, decided to buy him a ticket to Taormina. [paragraph] Francis said, "It	[	317.22–25	faltered; yet his faltering, like that change in his face, ought not to be dismay; for what could suit him better? All places that the eye of heaven visits are to the wise man ports and happy havens! [no paragraph] He said, "It
337.24–31	go—" [paragraph] This was the end of Lorna, of	[	317.26–32	go to Taormina." Habit made him pause cau-

	course; and for a moment, though so fortunate, Francis was in despair. He hung on the sharp tenterhook of desolation—*Since there's no help, come let us kiss and part*—taking a long vain look back. He said then, "I really think it might be best to leave as soon as possible. Before Walter settles down. This			tiously; but this time, what was there to worry about? It cost him a pang to have to want it; but this time what he wanted was also what (How fortunate! How fortunate he always was!) Mrs. Cunningham wanted. He smiled and said, "I think we should go as soon as possible. This
337.32	did	[	317.33	had
337.32–		[	317.33–	
338.1	expect quite such a full agreement. She gazed at		318.1	expected so cordial an agreement. She looked at
338.2	wouldn't	[	318.2	don't
338.3–6	Francis hardly trusted himself to speak. He tried smiling and shaking his head; but Mrs. Cunningham had asked a kind question, and to answer by signs was impolite. "I would be glad to go," Francis said.	[	318.3–5	The considerateness that used a form of asking ought to be acknowledged. "That's very kind of you," Francis said warmly. "But no, I would be glad to go."
338.8	hand-me-down .	[	318.7	shabby

A 11.2.b
Second English printing: London, New York & Toronto: Longmans, Green, [1948].

On copyright page: 'New Impression by lithography 1948'.

6s. The A. M. Heath records indicate that 533 copies were sold and that 4,939 were remaindered in 1952.

A 11.2.c
Third English printing: London, New York & Toronto: Longmans, Green, [1958].

On copyright page: 'Issued in this edition 1958'.

16s. 5,050 copies printed. The A. M. Heath records indicate that 2,798 copies were sold.

A 11.3
Third edition: Ask Me Tomorrow or The Pleasant Comedy of Young Fortunatus. New York: Harcourt, Brace & World, [1969].

"Uniform Edition." $6.95.

Collation: Substantive variants in the American editions:

Harcourt, Brace (1940)			Harcourt, Brace & World "Uniform Edition" (1969)
iii	*Ask Me Tomorrow*	[	vi	Ask Me Tomorrow | or The Pleasant Comedy of | Young Fortunatus

3.1–4.32	Even . . . living.	[		[omitted]
5.1–3	The hotel . . . big.	[	3.1–10	On a . . . large-sized.
5.4	Francis Ellery	[	3.10	Francis
5.4	an armchair	[	3.11	a big armchair
5.7	houses	[	3.14	house
6.19	day	[	5.4	night
7.10	God's	[	5.28	heaven's
8.11	nor	[	6.25	or
10.2	"Vi prego!"	[	8.17	*"Prego!"*
11.5	"Cosa dite?"	[	9.20	*"Cosa dice?"*
16.19	field	[	15.14	fields
17.4	rainy	[	15.26	rain-wet
17.23–24	and did a tailor out of what the dance cost.	[	16.15	and let his bills ride still another month.
21.9	distraught accessories-before-the-fact to	[	20.3–4	distraught principals in the second degree to
23.18–19	her. [paragraph] She	[	22.15	her. [no paragraph] She
25.27	deprecatingly	[	24.23	self-deprecatory
26.19–20	felt enough of a fancy	[	25.16	felt fancy enough
26.22	an	[	25.19	some
26.25	was balanced and sym-metrical	[	25.22	might be thought good by
28.22	took a little gingerly	[	27.22	gingerly took a little
28.22	drew	[	27.22	screwed
28.31	it carefully	[	28.1–2	the bottom
38.30	ordered dinner	[	38.4	asked for a menu
39.24	it; but he	[	38.30	it. He
43.11	plummeting to	[	42.20	plummeting from exhilara-tion to
49.6	*for Christ's sake*	[	48.24	*ask for it*
60.3	"O.K.,"	[	60.15	"Oh,"
61.15–16	skis." He did not. He	[	61.29–62.3	skis." He had not said it. His feeling about Walter's misfortune was too compli-cated. Trying to ignore it, he had been anxious to pretend that it did not ex-ist. He was unwilling to re-fer to it. Sympathetically, he did not want to show that he ever noticed it; but his sympathy was mixed with other feelings. He
65.13	very likely	[	66.2	probably
65.14	later	[	66.3	subsequently
67.6	rises. Not far	[	67.30	rises. Amid them and not far
68.23	decenter	[	69.11	more decent
68.26	remember	[	69.14	realize
68.27	be coming if	[	69.16	be to come if
69.16–17	judiciously	[	70.5–6	judicious
70.6	by boredom	[	70.28–29	by evident boredom

70.26	affection	[	71.17–18	affectionateness
70.30	the awful thing	[	71.21	the sad, sad thing
72.24	good a joke	[	73.16	exhilarating a jest
72.26	nor	[	73.18	or
73.5	anything	[	73.30	something
73.21	motormen's	[	74.14	motorman's
75.26	évités	[	76.22	*évitées*
82.12	Christiania	[	83.9	stem
82.20	sticks	[	83.17	poles
101.9	weight	[	102.18	weigh
105.12	pleasure. Violently	[	106.24	pleasure. Exhilarated, vio-lently
109.16	and almost closed	[	110.30	and closed
111.31– 112.1	said. [paragraph] Maggie	[	113.14–15	said. [no paragraph] Mag-gie
115.12	work," he observed.	[	116.31	work."
116.6–7	than as a	[	117.27	than a
118	[no section heading]	[	120	[section heading] I
121.4	wishing	[	123.13	wished
122.13–14	some dressed, some	[	124.26	some dressed for dinner, some
122.29	dinner	[	125.11	the evening
122.30	pinned at	[	125.12	pinned together at
124.5	their abhorrence of him or of America;	[	126.19–20	their distaste for the not quite-quite;
126.19	while	[	129.5	and
126.30	Wellesley. With	[	129.16–19	Wellesley. He remembered her crinkly blonde hair, the faintly husky tone of her voice, the tone of her skin, dusty, faintly freckled, about the same gold tone as her hair. With
129.15	cheerful	[	132.4	animated
130.16	affair	[	133.6	affairs
131.19	an	[	134.10	a
131.20–21	her up	[	134.12	her and up
132.25	on	[	135.17	in
133.14	never thought	[	136.6	never would have thought
152.1	she stopped herself,	[	154.21	she halted them halfway,
161.7	Aw	[	164.3	Ah
161.26	dismayed	[	164.23	amazed
162.19	Taken aback	[	165.17	Disconcerted
165	[no section number]	[	168	[section number] I
166.19	to judge	[	169.27	to be the judge of
166.23	senseless	[	170.1	foolish
166.31	Parker	[	170.9	Sargent
166.32	Jasper's	[	170.10	Jasper
167.2	Parker	[	170.12	Sargent
167.4	Parker	[	170.15	Sargent
172.2–3	dead. [paragraph] Francis	[	175.17	dead. [no paragraph] Francis

174.30	his	[	178.14	Francis's
175.18–19	he was left stultified	[	179.2	he stood discomfited
175.22	outbursts	[	179.5	extravagances
177.16	at the tyranny of impulse,	[	181.4–5	at angry impulse's blindness,
177.29	its	[	181.17	the
180.10–11	rhymes, all dancing	[	183.29	rhymes—dancing
185	[no section number]	[	188	[section number] I
187.6	fais	[	190.13	*vais*
198.8–9	and of man	[	201.23	and man
211.3	those	[	214.22	the
215.6	—willing to deceive, but incapable of deceit	[	218.27–28	—one willing to deceive, but too talentless to succeed
215.21	Aw	[	219.11	Ah
216.17–18	lessons ordinarily took	[	220.7	lessons took
219.10	Pettishly	[	223.3	Pettish
219.27	were	[	223.20	was
220.15	stay	[	224.8	keep
221.19	were	[	225.13	was
224.24	his other arm, and	[	228.16	his arm and
227	[no section number]	[	230	[section number] I
232.13	night	[	235.23	right
235.14	occupations	[	238.19	avocations
238.9	nor	[	241.10	or
238.10	nor	[	241.11	or
240.28	are	[	243.30	were
240.29	abandon	[	243.31	abandoned
240.29	strike	[	243.32	struck
241.13	pads grew in it	[	244.14	pads filled it
245.28	Francis	[	248.31	he
249.1	Monte Carlo and	[	252.1	Monte and
252.10–11	hard. [paragraph] "You're	[	255.12–13	hard. [no paragraph] "You're
253.5	doubt Lorna actually	[	256.7	doubt actually
256.1	he did	[	259.6	did he
256.19	So	[	259.25	Do
259	[no section number]	[	262	[section number] I
267.17	pre-emptorily	[	270.32	peremptorily
269.25	Chasseurs d'Alpine	[	273.4	Chasseurs Alpins
274.21–22	own. [paragraph] "Here,"	[	278.6	own. [no paragraph] "Here,"
274.23–24	lips. [paragraph] "And	[	278.7	lips. [no paragraph] "And
283.16–17	nobody told me about them	[	287.10–11	nobody mentioned them to me
287	[no section number]	[	290	[section number] I
288.19–20	move. [paragraph] "Walter	[	291.26–27	move. [no paragraph] "Walter
309.19	were	[	313.5	was
314.28	want to try one	[	318.24	want one
314.32	peddling	[	318.27	pedaling
319.5	on	[	323.3	in
325.22–23	doctor, whose manner	[	329.19–20	doctor, in his manner

325.24	intelligence, had been so	[	329.20–21	intelligence, so
326.5	grow	[	330.3	grown
329.3	her coat and hat still on	[	333.3	wearing her coat and hat still
329.18	quite	[	333.19	very
330.9–10	very much for not having told you more about it	[	334.6–7	a great deal for never having explained it to you
330.12	Francis said, "The	[	334.9	"Walter told me," said Francis. "The
330.16–17	It will be	[	334.13–14	It's going to be
332.1	of course	[	336.1	no doubt
332.13	friendly;	[	336.13–14	friendly to him;
332.19–20	which upset everything	[	336.20–21	which staggered and smashed things
333.6	lark.	[	337.9–11	lark. Gwen might allow that love laughed at locksmiths; but at common sense love would laugh over Gwen's dead body.
333.15	out.	[	337.20	out of it.
333.27	out and	[	338.1	out the door and
335.12–13	lounge. [paragraph] "If	[	339.14	lounge. [no paragraph] "If
337.17–		[	341.26–	
338.8			342.15	

337.17–338.8   "Well, it is so hard to tell. I think it might." [paragraph] Francis faltered; but he was, he remembered, always fortunate. When he wished, the wish came true. When he did not know what on earth to do, Mrs. Cunningham, all unaware, told him; and all unasked, decided to buy him a ticket to Taormina. [paragraph] Francis said, "It seems to me that if there is any chance at all that it would be better, we ought to go—" [paragraph] This was the end of Lorna, of course; and for a moment, though so fortunate, Francis was in despair. He hung on the sharp tenterhook of desolation—*Since there's no help, come let us kiss and part*—taking a long vain look back. He said then, "I really think it might be best to leave as

341.26–342.15   "Well, I think it might." [paragraph] Francis faltered; yet his faltering, like that change in his face, ought not to be dismay; for what could suit him better? All places that the eye of heaven visits are to the wise man ports and happy havens! He said, "It seems to me that if there is any chance that it would be better, we ought to go to Taormina." Habit made him pause cautiously; but this time what was there to worry about? It cost him a pang to have to want it; but this time what he wanted was also what (How fortunate! How fortunate he always was!) Mrs. Cunningham wanted. He smiled and said, "I think we should go as soon as possible. This week, if it can be arranged." [paragraph] Mrs. Cunningham had not, soon as possible. Before Walter settles down. This week, if it can be arranged." [paragraph] Mrs. Cunningham did not, perhaps, expect quite such a full agreement. She gazed at him with mild inquiry. She said, "You wouldn't mind leaving so soon, Francis?" [paragraph] Francis hardly trusted himself to speak. He tried smiling and shaking his head; but Mrs. Cunningham had asked a kind question, and to answer by signs was impolite. "I would be glad to go," Francis said. [paragraph] Out of the dining room came the maître de hotel, bustling and important in his hand-me-down dress clothes.

perhaps, expected so cordial an agreement. She looked at him with mild inquiry. She said, "You don't mind leaving so soon, Francis?" [paragraph] The considerateness that used a form of asking ought to be acknowledged. "That's very kind of you," Francis said warmly. "But no, I would be glad to go." [paragraph] Out of the dining room came the maître d'hôtel, bustling and important in his shabby dress clothes.

338.10   laying   [342.17   putting

A 11.4
Fourth edition: See *Just Representations,* B 30.

A 12 THE JUST AND THE UNJUST

A 12.1.a
First edition, first printing [1942]

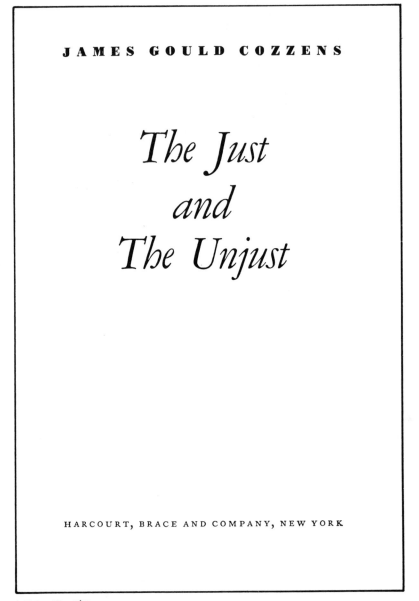

JAMES GOULD COZZENS

The Just
and
The Unjust

HARCOURT, BRACE AND COMPANY, NEW YORK

A 12.1.a: 8″ × 5½″

COPYRIGHT, 1942, BY

JAMES GOULD COZZENS

All rights reserved, including the right to reproduce this book or portions thereof in any form.

first edition

PRINTED IN THE UNITED STATES OF AMERICA

[i–x] [1–2] 3–5 [6] 7–434 [435–438]

[1–14]¹⁶

Contents: pp. i–ii: blank; p. iii: half title; p. iv: *'Other books by James Gould Cozzens' [SSSP, LA, M&B, AMT];* p. v.: title; p. vi: copyright; p. vii: 'To | EDWARD G. BIESTER | *Cuilibet in arte sua perito est credendum* | COKE ON LITTLETON, 125'; p. viii: blank; p. ix: epigraph; p. x: blank; p. 1: half title; p. 2: blank; pp. 3–5: 'RECORD'; p. 6: blank; pp. 7–434: text, headed *'One';* pp. 435–438: blank.

Typography and paper: 6" (6⁷⁄₁₆") × 3¹³⁄₁₆". 36 lines per page. Running heads: rectos and versos, 'THE JUST AND THE UNJUST'. Wove paper.

Binding: Black V cloth (smooth). Spine stamped in white: 'COZZENS | *The Just* | and | *The Unjust* | HARCOURT, BRACE | AND COMPANY | [broken rule]'. White wove endpapers. Top and bottom edges trimmed; fore-edge rough-trimmed. Top edge stained yellow.

Dust jacket: Front and spine brownish gray. Front: '[yellow] [rule] | JAMES GOULD | COZZENS | [black-and-white drawing of courthsoue square] | [yellow] THE JUST | AND THE | UNJUST | [rule]'. Spine: '[yellow] JAMES | GOULD | COZZENS | THE | JUST | AND THE | UNJUST | HARCOURT, BRACE | AND COMPANY | [rule]'. Back: photo of Cozzens and list of 6 of his novels. Front flap: price and blurb for *J&U.* Back flap: ad for war bonds and suggestion that the book be sent to a serviceman.

Publication: 25,000 copies of the first printing. Published 23 July 1942. $2.50. Copyright #A 166043.

Printing: Printed and bound by Quinn & Boden, Rahway, N.J.

Locations: LC (JUL-3 1942); Lilly (dj); MJB (dj).

Note 1: There is a copyright-page variant: 'PRINTED IN THE UNITED STATES OF AMERICA' and 'PRINTED AND BOUND IN THE UNITED STATES OF AMERICA | BY THE HADDON CRAFTSMEN, INC., CAMDEN, N. J.' The former appears on HB copies and the latter on BOMC copies (A 12.1.b and A 12.1.c). The one-line notice appears in the LC deposit copy.

Note 2: Abridged in *Omnibook,* IV (October 1942), 91–118.

A 12.1.b
Book-of-the-Month Club printing: New York: Harcourt, Brace, [1942].

On copyright page: 'first edition', with 2-line slug (see A 12.1.a, Note 1).

Dust jacket for A 12.1.a

August 1942 BOMC selection. 'S' at bottom of p. 434. Binding has broken rule on spine below 'AND COMPANY'. Dust jacket omits price on front flap and has BOMC seal on back.

Locations: Lilly (dj); MJB.

A 12.1.c
Book-of-the-Month Club reprint: New York: Harcourt, Brace, [1942].

The *'first edition'* slug was removed, but the 2-line printer's slug and the 'S' were retained. The 5 September 1942 *Publishers Weekly* reported: "250,000 copies have been printed including book club copies."

A 12.1.d
Harbrace Modern Classics printings: New York: Harcourt, Brace, [1950].

12 printings. Reprints noted: 'E.9.57', 'L.5.67'. Also noted without HBMC slug on title page and with 'W' on copyright page. Dual Book-of-the-Month Club alternate with *Guard of Honor* on December 1957.

A 12.1.e
Harvest printings: New York: Harcourt, Brace & World, [1965].

Harvest #HB 91. $1.95. Wrappers. 5 printings. Reprint noted: 'DEFGHIJ'.

Collation: Substantive variants in the American first-edition plates:*

Harcourt, Brace (1942)		Harvest Printing (1965)	
21.10–11	had been on the trail of Frederick Zollicoffer and his narcotics business for months	[21.10–12	was persuaded that Howell had been mixed up several years before in a mail robbery
21.18–20	them a good deal of trouble. But they knew that Howell had been involved with Zollicoffer and the drug traffic, and they meant to eliminate him, too.	[21.18–20	the authorities trouble. But an F.B.I. agent was shot in the investigation of that mail robbery and they meant to get everyone who might have been involved.
32.19	F.B.I. had been after him for months.	[32.19–20	Bureau of Narcotics was getting ready to grab him.
46.19	postmorten	[46.19	postmortem
85.34	The Federal Bureau of Investigation thinks so.	[85.34	We think so.
100.15	peddling	[100.15	pedaling
311.30	genuine	[311.30	effective

*Cozzens' revisions of the FBI material were made in response to a protest from J. Edgar Hoover.

A 12.2.a
First English edition, first printing [1943]

THE
JUST AND THE
UNJUST

by

JAMES GOULD COZZENS

Certainty is the Mother of Repose;
therefore the Law aims at Certainty.

LORD HARDWICKE

JONATHAN CAPE
THIRTY BEDFORD SQUARE
LONDON

A 12.2.a: 7½″ × 4¹⁵⁄₁₆″

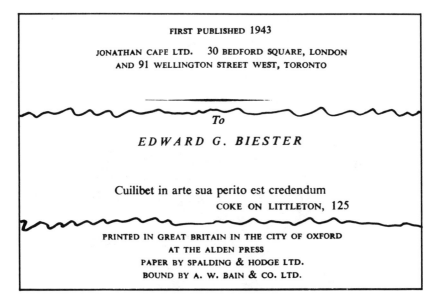

FIRST PUBLISHED 1943

JONATHAN CAPE LTD.   30 BEDFORD SQUARE, LONDON
AND 91 WELLINGTON STREET WEST, TORONTO

To

EDWARD G. BIESTER

Cuilibet in arte sua perito est credendum
COKE ON LITTLETON, 125

PRINTED IN GREAT BRITAIN IN THE CITY OF OXFORD
AT THE ALDEN PRESS
PAPER BY SPALDING & HODGE LTD.
BOUND BY A. W. BAIN & CO. LTD.

[1–4] 5–319 [320]

[A] B–I K–U⁸

Contents: p. 1: half title; p. 2: *'By the same Author'* [*Castaway, COF, M&B*]; p. 3: title; p. 4: copyright; pp. 5–6: 'RECORD'; pp. 7–320: text, headed 'ONE | 1'.

Typography and paper: 5¾″ (5¹⁵⁄₁₆″) × 3³⁄₁₆″. 42 lines per page. No running heads. Wove paper.

Binding: Strong red (#12) V cloth (smooth). Front: 'THE JUST AND THE UNJUST'. Spine: 'THE JUST | AND THE | UNJUST | [decorated rule] | JAMES | GOULD | COZ-ZENS | [JC flower-urn device]'. White wove endpapers. Top and fore-edges trimmed; bottom edge rough-trimmed.

Dust jacket: Front and spine orange. Front: '[black] JAMES GOULD COZZENS | [black on white panel with black and white arrow pointing from right] THE | JUST | [outside panel] AND [white] THE | [white on black panel with black and white arrow pointing from left] UN | JUST | [white script on black notched panel] Book Society Fiction Choice.' Spine: '[black] JAMES | GOULD | COZZENS | [black and white arrow pointing down] | [white on black panel] THE | JUST | [black on white] AND | [white on black] THE | [black on white panel] UN | JUST | [outside panel] [JC flower-urn device]'. Back is blank white. Front flap: blurb for *J&U*. Back flap: announcement for the BBC.

Publication: Unknown number of copies of the first English printing. Published 12 April 1943. 9/6. The A. M. Heath records indicate that 12,296 copies were sold.

Printing: See copyright page.

Locations: BL (31 MAR '43); MJB (dj).

Collation: Substantive variants between the first American edition and the first English edition:

Dust jacket for A 12.2.a

Harcourt, Brace (1942)			Cape (1943)	
21.16	F.B.I. agents	[	17.30	F.B.I. (Federal Bureau of Investigation) agents
46.19	postmorten	[	36.10	postmortem
59.29	did you get	[	46.4	did get
100.15	peddling	[	75.18	pedalling
125.20	defendant.	[	93.41	defendant?
181.33	curb	[	135.35	kerb
202.30	curb	[	150.35	kerb
234.19	whether	[	173.42	wherhet
264.15	Sam	[	195.9	Abner
267.31	he	[	197.28	she
267.31	she	[	197.28	he
287.35	So we	[	212.25	Sowe
300.25	curb	[	221.39	kerb
309.22	bored	[	228.19	bore
323.21	Mapes	[	239.2	Napes
424.8	sneaker	[	312.28	rubber shoe

A 12.2.b
Second English printing: London: Cape, [1943].

On copyright page: 'SECOND IMPRESSION APRIL 1943'.

A 12.2.c
Third English printing: London, New York & Toronto: Longmans, Green, [1958].

3,050 copies printed. The A. M. Heath records indicate that 1,850 copies were sold.

A 12.3
Australian edition: Sydney & London: Angus & Robertson, 1943.

On copyright page: 'Set up, printed and bound | in Australia by | Halstead Press Pty Limited | 9–19 Nickson Street, Sydney | 1943'.

The A. M. Heath records indicate that 3,450 copies were sold.

Locations: Australian National University Library; National Library of Australia.

A 13 TECHNIQUE IN WEATHER
Only printing (1943)

TECHNICAL ORDER NO. 30-100D-1

INSTRUMENT FLYING

TECHNIQUE

IN

WEATHER

NOTICE: *This document contains information affecting the National Defense of the United States within the meaning of the Espionage Act, 50 U.S.C., 31 and 32, as amended. Its transmission or the revelation of its contents in any manner to an unauthorized person is prohibited by law.*

PUBLISHED BY AUTHORITY OF THE COMMANDING GENERAL,
ARMY AIR FORCES, BY THE HEADQUARTERS,
AIR SERVICE COMMAND, PATTERSON FIELD, FAIRFIELD, OHIO

JUNE 1, 1943

A 13: $10\frac{7}{8}'' \times 8\frac{1}{2}''$

[a] A I–II 1–70 [71–72]

[1]³⁸

Contents: p. a: title; p. A: restriction statement and 'DISTRIBUTION NOTE'; p. I: contents; p. II: 'Foreword'; pp. 1–70: text, headed 'Section I'; pp. 71–72: blank.

Typography and paper: 8⅞" (9⅝") × 7¹⁄₁₆". Double-columned. Running heads: rectos and versos, section number and 'RESTRICTED | T. O. No. 30-100D-1'. Wove paper.

Binding: Light greenish blue paper covers. Front: 'INSTRUMENT FLYING | [inside brace] [slanted script] Technique | in | Weather | [Army Air Force insignia within black circle]'. Stapled.

Publication.   Unknown number of copies distributed gratis. Released 1 June 1943.

Printing: Unknown.

Location: MJB.

Note: Cozzens collaborated on this manual with E. J. Minser, chief meteorologist of TWA, and others in 1942–1943. Minser's "Look to Weather Elements for Successful Flight," *Air Transport,* I (October 1943), 32–37, has this editorial note: "AIR TRANSPORT is proud to present Mr. Minser's articles and the illustrations made available by ASC and the Training Aids Division of the AAF. Incidentally, the Training Aids and Flying Safety Divisions, AAF, collaborated with Mr. Minser in a book, featuring the pilot 'Scratchy,' on weather flying for Army pilots."

Front cover for A 13

A 14 AIRWAYS FLYING
Only printing (1943)

A 14: rectangular panel in blue; 10″ × 7½″

[1–32]

16 leaves, stapled.

Contents: p. 1: title; p. 2: 'FOREWORD'; pp. 3–31: text, headed 'CLEARANCE'; p. 32: blank.

Binding: Paper covers printed in white, black, and shades of blue and gray. Front '[high-flying plane with zigzag line leading to ground, with city and rivers] | [at bottom in white on black panel] airways | flying | [at right] *A HANDBOOK* | *FOR MILITARY* | *PILOTS'*. Back: blue eagle and triangle within black circle on blue panel. Stapled through left margin.

Publication: Unknown number of copies distributed gratis. Released October 1943.

Printing: Unknown.

Location: Albert F. Simpson Historical Research Center, Maxwell AFB, Ala. (143.512 D).

Note: An editorial note with "Airways Flying" (see C 79) explains: "Capt. Cozzens and Mr. Moore are also the authors of a new book *Airways Flying.* . . . The Training Aids Division of the Air Forces assigned Capt. Cozzens to collaborate in preparing the book with CAA's Bert Moore and Capt. L. N. Conklin of the Flying Safety Division, Flight Control Command."

Front cover for A 14

A 15 GUARD OF HONOR

A 15.1.a
First edition, first printing [1948]

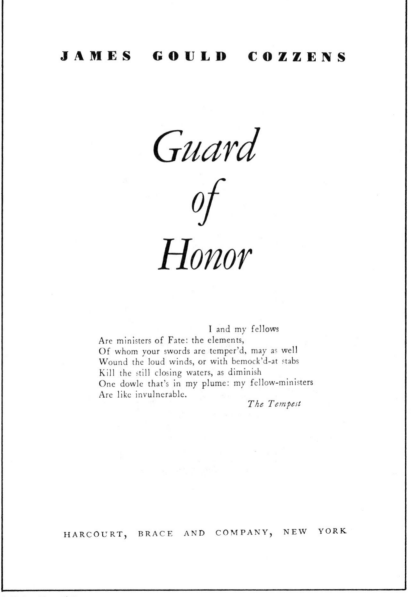

JAMES   GOULD   COZZENS

Guard

of

Honor

I and my fellows
Are ministers of Fate: the elements,
Of whom your swords are temper'd, may as well
Wound the loud winds, or with bemock'd-at stabs
Kill the still closing waters, as diminish
One dowle that's in my plume: my fellow-ministers
Are like invulnerable.

The Tempest

HARCOURT,   BRACE   AND   COMPANY,   NEW   YORK

A 15.1.a: 8″ × 5½″

[i–vi] [1–2] 3–88 [89–90] 91–285 [286–288] 289–631 [632–634]

[1–20]¹⁶

Contents: p. i: half title; p. ii: *'by the same author' [J&U, AMT, M&B, Castaway, LA, SSSP, SOP];* p. iii: title; p. iv: copyright; p. v: contents; p. vi: blank; p. 1: 'ONE | THURSDAY'; p. 2: blank; pp. 3–631: text; pp. 632–634: blank.

Typography and paper: 6¹⁵⁄₁₆″ (7⅛″) × 4″. 37 lines per page. No running heads. Wove paper.

Binding: Medium gray (#265) V cloth (smooth). Spine stamped in blue: 'COZZENS | Guard | of | Honor | HARCOURT, BRACE | AND COMPANY'. White wove endpapers. Top and bottom edges trimmed.

Dust jacket: Front and spine graduated from dark blue at top to gray at bottom. Front: '[white and black] GUARD | OF | HONOR | [heraldic design of armor and pikes] | [Liberator bomber] | [converging lines] | [white] JAMES GOULD COZZENS'. Spine: '[white] [script] Cozzens | [roman] GUARD | OF | HONOR | [script] Harcourt, Brace | and Company'. Back: photo of Cozzens and 5 blurbs about him. Front flap has blurb for *GOH,* continued on back flap. Also copies with yellow wraparound band printed in black. Front: 'PULITZER | PRIZE NOVEL | 1949'. Spine: 'PULITZER | PRIZE | NOVEL | 1949'. Back has 3 blurbs.

Publication: 12,500 copies of the first printing. $3.50. Published 30 September 1948. Copyright #A 26744.

Printing: Printed and bound by Quinn & Boden, Rahway, N.J.

Locations: LC (OCT 25 1948); MJB (dj and with wraparound band).

Review copy: Bound copy with printed pale gray green slip pasted on free front endpaper: '[black] ADVANCE COPY | FROM HARCOURT, BRACE AND COMPANY | Please note the release date for review and the price | [stamped in light blue green] SEP 30 1948 PRICE $350'. *Location:* MJB.

A 15.1.b
Second printing: New York: Harcourt, Brace, 1949.

Not seen. 3,000 copies.

A 15.1.c
Third printing: New York: Harcourt, Brace, 1949.

Not seen. 5,000 copies.

Dust jacket for A 15.1.a

A 15.1.d
First edition, first English printing (1949)

JAMES GOULD COZZENS

Guard

of

Honour

LONGMANS, GREEN AND CO
LONDON   NEW YORK   TORONTO

A 15.1.d: 7¼″ × 4¹³⁄₁₆″

[i–viii] [1–2] 3–88 [89–90] 91–285 [286–288] 289–631 [632]

[A] B–I K–U^{16}

Contents: pp. i–ii: blank; p. iii: half title; p. iv: *'by the same author' [J&U, AMT, M&B, Castaway, LA, SSSP, SOP];* p. v: title; p. vi: copyright; p. vii: contents; p. viii: epigraph; p. 1: 'ONE | THURSDAY'; p. 2: blank; pp. 3–631: text; p. 632: blank.

Typography and paper: Same as first Harcourt, Brace printing.

Binding: Deep blue (#179) V cloth (smooth). Spine goldstamped: 'GUARD | OF | HONOUR | [rule] | J. G. | COZZENS | LONGMANS'. White wove endpapers. All edges trimmed.

Dust jacket: Front and spine light blue. Front: '[white] GUARD OF | HONOUR | [4 pursuit planes in white, dark red, and blue over airfield] | [dark red] JAMES GOULD COZZENS'. Spine: '[pursuit plane] | [white] GUARD | of | HONOUR | [pursuit plane] | [dark red] JAMES | GOULD | COZZENS | [pursuit plane] | [white] LONGMANS'. Back: blurbs for *GOH* and Cozzens in red and blue. Front flap: *'For description of this book | see back of jacket* | [price]'. Back flap: *'Printed in Great Britain'.*

Publication: 5,100 copies of the first English printing. Published 7 November 1949. 12/6. The A. M. Heath records indicate that 4,925 copies were sold, but the Brandt & Brandt records state that 8,973 copies were sold in England and 8,697 were exported. A 1951 Longmans "Cheap Edition" sold 1,437 copies in 1951. This "Cheap Edition" was probably a new binding of the first-printing sheets.

Printing: See copyright page.

Locations: BL (7 NOV '49); MJB (dj).

Collation: Substantive variants between the first American printing and the first English printing:

Harcourt, Brace (1948)		Longmans, Green (1949)	
24.33	often do much to determine	[24.33	often determine
25.5–6	Headquarters, which handled	[25.5–6	Headquarters, whose Training Literature Section handled

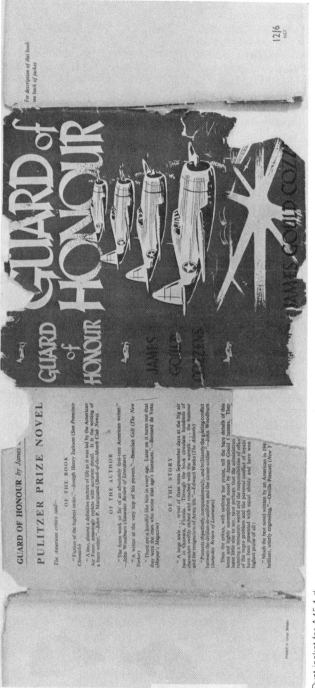

Dust jacket for A 15.1.d

27.37–28.1	ago, such decisions were	[	27.37–38	ago, decisions like this were
28.3	objections, disliking	[	28.2	objections; but disliking
28.3–4	If Nathaniel Hicks fussed enough, he might	[	28.3–4	If enough fuss was made, Major Whitney might
28.4–5	to the colonel, where it would run up against the directive. Prepare	[	28.4–5	to Colonel Coulthard. There they met the directive. Never mind! Prepare
28.8	firm	[	28.8	constant
28.8	The dismaying sense of it,	[	28.8–9	A dismaying sense of such pressure,
28.9–10	the various feelings of several million men caught up in a war	[	28.9–10	in the feelings of many million men at war
28.11	oppressed	[	28.11	weighed on
28.11	It	[	28.11	War
28.12	and reasoned	[	28.12	and upset reasoned
28.12–13	Pulled constantly up in blank amazement, a	[	28.13	Constantly halted, blankly amazed, a
28.28	had always	[	28.29–30	always had
29.12–14	at the captain's bars reflecting the dim light beyond the open door, on the collar of his shirt, hung on a chair with his folded trousers—preposterous	[	29.12–15	at his clothes hung on a chair; at the dark shape of the Air Force patch on the shirt's left sleeve, at the captain's bars reflecting the dim light beyond the open door—preposterous
30.5–6	Operations rather shyly	[	30.5–6	Operations shyly
34.6	himself nervously back	[	34.6	himself back
34.8–9	said somewhat uncertainly.	[	34.7	said.
34.15–16	them anxiously on	[	34.13–14	them on
43.23	plane a moment.	[	43.23	plane.
43.27	beside each one you	[	43.27	beside a lot of them you
46.5	the gray	[	46.5	the distant gray
46.5–6	Mexico far to the right faded	[	46.5–6	Mexico dimmed slowly, faded
46.7	character in a vast plane of shadow.	[	46.7	character.
46.10	eight thousand, five hundred	[	46.10	eight thousand five hundred
46.18	but only	[	46.18–19	but no masks and only
46.30	Beal good-naturedly.	[	46.30	Beal.
46.34	said critically.	[	46.34	said.
46.37	other, sure and contented in	[	46.37	other, at home in
50.22–23	spite of the	[	50.22–23	spite of it, and of the
50.28	with an entire faithfulness	[	50.28–29	with faithfulness
51.13–14	been busy that much longer rooting out the vestiges	[	51.13–14	been continuously busy rooting out vestiges

51.18	Unfortunately, when	[	51.18	It took time to see that when
51.18–19	end, you found all	[	51.18–19	end, all
51.19	it inherent	[	51.19	it must be inherent
51.19	In short, the first	[	51.19	That first
51.20	up that mess	[	51.20	up a mess
51.21	The new prudence	[	51.20	Increased prudence
52.1–2	It was only necessary for Colonel Ross to do it for him.	[	52.1–2	Colonel Ross had only to feel it incumbent on him to do some extra work.
116.27	a little nod	[	116.27	a nod
132.22	said benevolently:	[	132.22	said:
133.38	of uneasy strain	[	133.38	of strain
134.6	this little dilemma	[	134.6	this dilemma
145.27–33	irritably. [paragraph] While Lieutenant Pettie got out, Captain Duchemin stood regarding Captain An- drews with a surprised but happy smile. "Brains?" he said. "Who dat?" He be- gan to shake with new chuckles. "No brains at all," he chanted, "no brains at all! She married a man who had no—" [paragraph]The	[	145.30–31	irritably. [paragraph] The
199.34	said calmly:	[	199.34	said:
204.22	hand reflectively.	[	204.22	hand.
209.12	said icily:	[	209.12	said:
236.7–8	head and said:	[	236.7–8	head. He said:
239.13	Giving it no heed, Colonel	[	239.13	Colonel
240.34–35	where earthbanks had been piled to form butts,	[	240.34–35	where piled earthbanks formed butts,
241.2–3	area. [paragraph] On	[	241.2	area. [no paragraph] On
241.3–4	way several painters	[	241.3	way painters
241.9–10	and a variety of disem- bodied voices constantly filled	[	241.9–10	and disembodied voices filled
241.12	Murphy, staring with	[	241.12	Murphy. Both stared with
241.26–27	marks and were jostling around, arranging	[	241.26	marks and were arranging
241.32–34	microphones in answer to the medley of voices that came and went on the	[	241.32–33	microphones, answering voices that came and went through the
241.36	drawl went on:	[	241.36	drawl proceeded:
242.30	want to come in.	[	242.31	want in.
243.24	major let his lifted baton fall;	[	243.24	major's suspended baton fell;
245.10	said slowly:	[	245.10	said:

245.19	course, I realize that when	[	245.19	course, when
249.3	year there is an	[	249.3	year we have an
249.4–5	transcript of the conversa-tion.	[	249.4–5	transcript.
249.5–6	was told to repeat	[	249.5	was to repeat
250.26	Baxter, benevolent, beam-ing	[	250.26	Baxter, beaming
251.9	said cheerfully.	[	251.9	said.
254.26–27	including, it seemed, that	[	254.26–27	including that
254.32	cover them over.	[	254.32	cover those facts over.
255.37	said gravely,	[	255.37	said,
264.8	—purification by	[	264.8	—ordering by
266.1	moved again,	[	266.1	moved,
266.13	moving black faces	[	266.13	moving faces
278.14	able	[	278.14	unable
278.25	himself down on it heavily.	[	278.25	himself sink on it.
282.14–21	knows. He is wrong, of course. Either you see why, or you don't. It is a matter of falsifying a rela-tionship, which has to be a kind of common trust, be-tween two people. If he is, in the very exact phrase, untrue, and she doesn't know it, he may think he's getting away with some-thing. He isn't. He has made it no longer a com-mon trust. He's made an unstable arrangement of ignorance on one side and deceit on the other. How-ever,	[	282.14	knows. However,
289.32	have this morning.	[	289.32	have.
314.11–12	shoes! I guess the wicked are still fleeing when no man pursueth. The	[	314.11	shoes! The
322.28	said. "What are they doing to Bus? You	[	322.28	said. "You
323.14	said woefully:	[	323.14–15	said in a woeful voice:
323.16	Ross, still unnerved, no-ticed	[	323.17	Ross noticed
323.27–28	marching the three pla-toons of a Negro	[	323.28	marching a Negro
324.3	his gleaming black	[	324.3	his youthful black
324.28	up there and	[	324.28	up and
327.13	said curiously:	[	327.13	said:
341.15	[paragraph] "He says too much," Colonel	[	341.15	[paragraph] Colonel
381.14	status	[	381.14–15	condition

383.28	get	[	383.28	find
404.13	when	[	404.13	as
420.27–28	twenty-five	[	420.27	many
427.11	said amiably.	[	427.11	said.
458.1–4	[paragraph] "Four-thirty?" Captain Duchemin said archly. "Oh! You mean: one six three zero! Didn't understand you for a moment! Can do, Major!" [paragraph] Major	[	458.1	[paragraph] Major
483.12	can tell me when	[	483.12	can see I hear when
483.18–20	Understand?" [paragraph] "Yes, sir," Sergeant Olmstead said, appalled. [paragraph] "All	[	483.19–20	Understand?" [paragraph] "All
492.19–20	there could even understand	[	492.19–20	there was even soldier enough to understand
494.34– 495.3	does." [paragraph] The tone, so unmistakably that of testy impotence, baffled Captain Collins. One look at Colonel Coulthard showed that this angry, vain floundering was far removed from his nature and habit. Restraining influences, to which he submitted with the worst possible grace, were laid on him. Captain Collins, blinking through his glasses, looked away. [paragraph] Much	[	494.36– 495.1	does." [paragraph] Much
495.23–24	I was there, but I had nothing to do with any	[	495.21–22	I didn't arrange any
507.7–8	telling what General Beal may do with the	[	507.7–8	telling about the general and the
532.18–19	Except for Pop, who had the stoicism of the slow-witted, he was the oldest man;	[	532.18–19	He was the oldest man here;
548.7	they	[	548.7	some
548.8	then	[	548.8	some
548.9	They	[	548.9	Others
553.26–27	ring, perhaps pondering what	[	553.26–27	ring. Not impossibly he pondered what
553.33	faint	[	553.33	mild
559.3	said drily.	[	559.3	said.
563.15	became abruptly aware	[	563.15	became aware

569.36	went trotting off	[	569.36	went off
581.25–27	said. "I know the ropes here." Perhaps he was again making a favorable impression on himself—the dextrous manager; the man with a way with him. He said: "You	[	581.28	said. "You
582.1–2	said. "He has his uses. I	[	582.1	said. "I
583.29–30	there sagely, looking	[	583.29–30	there, looking
586.37	anyone	[	586.37	everybody
586.38	if ever anyone was)	[	586.38–587.1	if a human being ever was)
587.2–3	this, put themselves alone together in privacy, they	[	587.2–3	this, privately put themselves alone together, they
588.31–32	said. [paragraph] In	[	588.31–33	said. [paragraph] He hoped Katherine would have a good night. [paragraph] In
589.1–2	He hoped Katherine would have a good night. Standing listless under the shower, Nathaniel	[	589.1–2	Turning on the shower, standing listless under it, Nathaniel

A 15.1.e
Second English printing: London, New York & Toronto: Longmans, Green, 1950.

Not seen. The Longmans records show that 2,990 copies were printed.

A 15.1.f
Trade reprints: New York: Harcourt, Brace, [   ].

Printings noted: 'H.10.57', 'J.11.65', and no slug on copyright page.

A 15.1.g
Book-of-the-Month Club reprint: New York: Harcourt, Brace, [1957].

On copyright page: 'W'.

Dual BOMC alternate with *The Just and The Unjust* in December 1957. Dark blue dot on back cover. Dust jacket replaced publisher's imprint on front flap with notice of Pulitzer Prize. Back of jacket has blurbs by *Infantry Journal,* Miller, Woodburn, and Paterson.

A 15.1.h
Third English printing: London, New York & Toronto: Longmans, Green, [1958].

On copyright page: 'Issued in this edition 1958'.

5,025 copies. The A. M. Heath records indicate that 2,206 copies were sold

A 15.1.i
Harvest printings: New York: Harcourt, Brace & World, [1964].

On copyright page: 'A.8.64'.

Harvest #HB 77. $2.45. Wrappers. 5 printings. Reprint noted: '[DEFGH].

Collation: Substantive variants in the American first-edition plates:*

Harcourt, Brace (1948)		Harvest Printing (1964)	
85.24	Lieutenant Carricker	[85.24–25	Lieutenant Colonel Car-ricker
102.3	slightly	[102.3	slightingly
244.7	orchestra	[244.7	orchestral
293.4	Hick's	[293.4	Hicks's
318.20–21	moment (though for them it was still yesterday) Fifth	[318.20	moment Fifth
450.35	has	[450.35	have
491.18	were	[491.18	was
532.18–19	not. Except for Pop, who had the stoicism of the slow-witted, he was the oldest man	[532.18–19	not. He was the oldest man here
549.33	NICHOLAS	[549.33	NICHOLS

A 15.2
Second edition: New York: Permabooks, [1952].

#P 148. 35¢. Wrappers.

A 15.3
Third edition: Franklin Center, Pa.: Franklin Library, 1978.

Sold by subscription.

---

*There are 111 alterations in the first-edition plates, most of which restyle numbers (for example, B-26 [B-Twenty-six) or restyle military acronyms (for example, WAC [Wac).

A 16.1.a₁
First edition, first printing, first state [1957]

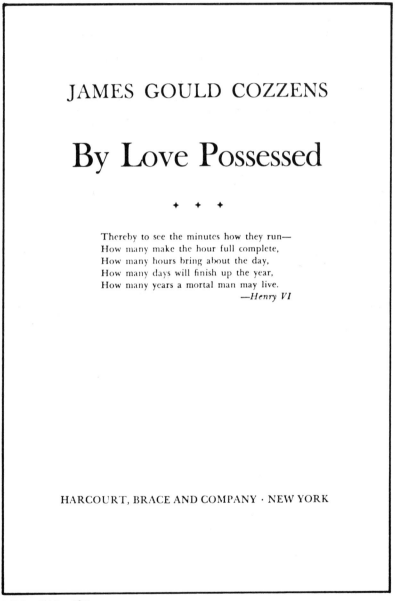

A 16.1.a: 8¹⁄₁₆″ × 5³⁄₈″

[i–vi] [1–2] 3–266 [267–268] 269–500 [501–502] 503–570

$[1-18]^{16}$. Lines 18 and 19 on p. 173 and lines 6 and 7 on p. 302 are transposed in the first state.

Contents: p. 1: half title; p. ii: *'Books by James Gould Cozzens'* [SSSP, LA, Castaway, M&B, AMT, J&U, GOH, BLP]; p. iii: title; p. iv: copyright; p. v: contents; p. vi: blank; p. 1: 'PART ONE | DRUMS AFAR OFF'; p. 2: blank; pp. 3–570: text, headed 'ONE'.

Typography and paper: 6⅛" (6⅜") × 4". 37 lines per page. No running heads. Wove paper.

Binding: Goldstamped deep blue (#179) V cloth (smooth). Front has clock. Spine: 'BY LOVE | POSSESSED | [row of 5 diamonds] | JAMES GOULD | COZZENS | HARCOURT, BRACE | AND COMPANY'. White wove endpapers. All edges trimmed.

Dust jacket: Printed on white. Front: '[red] BY LOVE | POSSESSED | [blue] JAMES GOULD | COZZENS | [gilt clock with 'OMNIA VINCIT AMOR' beneath face]'. Spine: '[vertically] BY LOVE POSSESSED | [orange] Harcourt, Brace | and Company | [yellow] JAMES GOULD COZZENS'. Back repeats front. Front flap: price and blurb for *BLP.* Back flap lists 7 books by JGC.

Publication: 50,000 copies of the first printing. Published 26 August 1957. $5.00. Copyright #A 298977.

Printing: Printed and bound by Colonial Press, Clinton, Mass.

Location: William Jovanovich.

A 16.1.a$_2$

First edition, first printing, second state (1957)
$[1-5]^{16}$ $[6]^{16}$ $(\pm 6_{10})$ $[7-9]^{16}$ $[10]^{16}$ $(\pm 10_{10})$ $[11-18]^{16}$; pp. 173–174 and 301–302 are cancels to correct transposed lines.

Locations: Lilly (dj); MJB (dj); Univ. of Virginia (dj, with review slip). LC deposit copy missing.

A 16.1.b

Trade reprints: New York: Harcourt, Brace, [1957].

Printings noted: 'B.8.57' (42,000), 'C.9.57' (50,000), 'D.9.57' (50,000), 'E.9.57' (50,000).

Dust jacket for A 16.1.a

A 16.1.c

Book-of-the-Month Club reprints: New York: Harcourt, Brace, [1957].

On copyright page: 'W'. Later BOMC printings omit the 'W'.

September 1957 BOMC selection. BOMC printings replace *'fuck'* with a dash at 507.13. Blindstamped dot at lower right on back cover. Dust jacket replaces price on front flap with BOMC notice.

Locations: BOMC, MJB.

A 16.1.d
First edition, first English printing (1958)

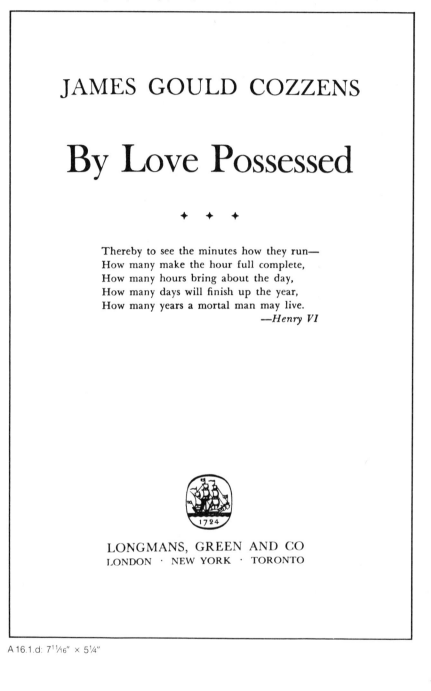

JAMES GOULD COZZENS

By Love Possessed

✦ ✦ ✦

Thereby to see the minutes how they run—
How many make the hour full complete,
How many hours bring about the day,
How many days will finish up the year,
How many years a mortal man may live.
                                    —*Henry VI*

LONGMANS, GREEN AND CO
LONDON · NEW YORK · TORONTO

A 16.1.d: 7¹¹⁄₁₆″ × 5¼″

Same pagination as Harcourt, Brace printing.

[A] B–I K–S^{16}.

Contents: Same as Harcourt, Brace printing, except that p. i has ad for *BLP*.

Typography and paper: Same as Harcourt, Brace printing.

Binding: Goldstamped deep reddish orange (#36) paper-covered boards with V pattern (smooth). Front: '[facsimile signature] James Gould Cozzens'. Spine: '[on black panel] BY LOVE | POSSESSED | [tapered rule] | JAMES | GOULD | COZZENS | [below panel] LONGMANS'. White wove endpapers. All edges trimmed.

Dust jacket: Printed on white. Front: '[red] BY LOVE | POSSESSED | [black] JAMES GOULD | COZZENS | [gilt clock with "OMNIA VINCIT AMOR" at base, signed 'Philip Gough']'. Spine: '[vertically] BY LOVE POSSESSED [red] Longmans | JAMES GOULD COZZENS'. Back: '[in black and red] *Some American Press Opinions of* | BY LOVE POSSESSED | [9 excerpts]'. Front and back flaps in red and black. Front flap: blurb for *BLP*. Back flap: note on Cozzens.

Publication: 30,200 copies of the first English printing. Published 14 April 1958. 18s. The A. M. Heath records indicate that 48,899 copies of the English printings were sold.

Printing: See copyright page.

Locations: BL (21 FEB 58); Lilly (dj); MJB (dj).

Review copy: Signatures perfect bound in unprinted grayish brown (#61) wrappers. *Location:* MJB.

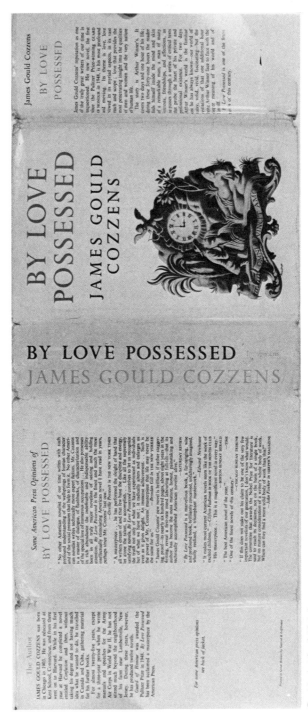

BY LOVE POSSESSED
JAMES GOULD COZZENS

BY LOVE POSSESSED
JAMES GOULD COZZENS

James Gould Cozzens

BY LOVE
POSSESSED

James Gould Cozzens' reputation as one of the truly great writers of our time is unquestioned. His new novel, the first since the Pulitzer Prize-winning GUARD OF HONOUR in 1948, is his most profound and moving. Its theme is love, love viewed in its myriad aspects, in its vast reach and scope; love that provides the most penetrating insight into the qualities of men and women and the very nature of human life.

The story is Arthur Winner's. It covers two days and one hour of his life; during those forty-nine hours the reader finds himself inside the mind and skin of a remarkable man, a man of many conceits, friendships, and affections, as it passes through a series of crises at the heart of his private and professional existence. For two days Arthur Winner's world is the familiar one he has always known—our world of today, solid, vivid, fascinating—but the relations of that one additional hour give it, Arthur Winner face to face with the true meaning of his world and of ...

By Love Possessed is one of the finest ... s of this century.

The Author

JAMES GOULD COZZENS was born in Chicago in 1903. He was educated at Kent School, Connecticut, and from there went on to Harvard. While in his first year at Harvard he completed a novel entitled *Confusion* and then, without taking his degree and not having much idea what he wanted to do, he travelled in Canada and Cuba, gathering material for his further books.

For almost twenty-five years, except for a three-year period when he wrote manuals and speeches for the Army Air Corps in World War II, he has not stirred much beyond the neighbourhood of his farm near Lambertville, New Jersey. During these years, however, he has produced twelve novels.

Guard of Honour was awarded the Pulitzer Prize in 1948. *By Love Possessed* has been acclaimed a masterpiece by the American Press.

For some American press opinions see back of jacket.

Some American Press Opinions of
BY LOVE POSSESSED

"No other American novelist of our time writes with such profound understanding of the workings of human character and of the social pressures that help to form it. No other American novelist writes technically more expert fiction. Mr. Cozzens is a master of dialogue, of flashbacks, of characterization and of the special lore of numerous occupations ... He also possesses in rich abundance the indefinable and indispensable ability born in all truly major novelists of seizing and holding attention. *By Love Possessed* is the finest and much the most intellectually stimulating American novel I have read in years, perhaps since Mr. Cozzens's last one."
—*Orville Prescott in* THE NEW YORK TIMES

"A masterpiece ... he has performed the sleight of hand that all writers dream of and that few have the discipline and energy, let alone the talent, to accomplish. ... Like all the supremely satisfying novels, *By Love Possessed* continues to let us recognize the truth not only of what we have experienced as individuals but of what we have not; it radically alters and enlarges us even as it gives delight. An immense achievement. ... Such is the power of Mr. Cozzens' masterpiece: this life may never be the same for us."
—*Brendan Gill in* THE NEW YORKER

"*By Love Possessed* is a marvellous book, a far-ranging, wise and profound book, brilliantly conceived, unfalteringly imagined, wholly realized, a triumphant masterwork."
—SATURDAY REVIEW

"It makes most current American novels seem like the work of excited children." —*Edward Newhouse*

"James Gould Cozzens' new novel is brilliant, if rather staggering proof—its nearly six hundred pages cover about eight years of living, reveal a first-rate mind labouring at full-tilt—that its author has become the most mature, honest, painstaking and technically accomplished American novelist."
—*Clifton Fadiman,* BOOK-OF-THE-MONTH CLUB

"His masterpiece. ... This is a magnificent novel in every way."
—BOSTON SUNDAY HERALD

"The best American novel of the year."
—TIME

"One of the finest novels of this century."
—CHICAGO SUNDAY TRIBUNE

"If this does not stake out his claim to be one of the very few important novelists of our generation I don't know what would. The committee that awards the Nobel Prize for literature is said to reach its decisions, not on the basis of a single book, but on mature consideration of a writer's whole body of work. Where can they find a more solid body of work than this?"
—*John Fischer in* HARPER'S MAGAZINE

Printed in Great Britain by Garrod & Lofthouse

Collation: No textual alterations have been found in the first English printing of *By Love Possessed.*

A 16.1.e
Second English printing: London, New York & Toronto: Longmans, Green, [1958].

On copyright page: 'Second impression 1958'. 5,000 copies.

A 16.1.f
Third English printing: London, New York & Toronto: Longmans, Green, [1958].

On copyright page: 'Third impression 1958'. 10,000 copies.

A 16.1.g
Fourth English printing: London, New York & Toronto: Longmans, Green, [1958].

On copyright page: 'Fourth impression 1958'. 10,000 copies.

A 16.1.h
Harvest printing: New York: Harcourt, Brace & World, [1967].

Harvest #HB 124. $2.95. Wrappers.

Collation: Substantive variants in the American first-edition plates:*

Harcourt, Brace (1957)		Harvest Printing (1967)		
97.9	horde	[	97.9	hoard
401.34	four	[	401.34	five

A 16.2
Second edition: Greenwich, Conn.: Fawcett, [1959].

Crest #t326. 75¢. Wrappers. Reprinted 5 times, 1961–1978.

A 16.3
Third edition: [Harmondsworth:] Penguin, [1960].

#1464. 5s. Wrappers. Reprinted 1961. The A. M. Heath records indicate that 33,181 copies were sold.

A 16.4
Fourth edition: Reader's Digest Condensed Books. Pleasantville, N.Y.: Readers's Digest Association, [1957].

Volume 4, Autumn Selections.

A 16.5
Fifth edition: Reader's Digest Condensed Books. London, Sydney & Cape Town: Reader's Digest Association, [1960].

The A. M. Heath records indicate that 669,781 copies were sold.

*There are 7 alterations in the first-edition plates.

A 17 CHILDREN & OTHERS

A 17.1.a
First edition, first printing [1964]

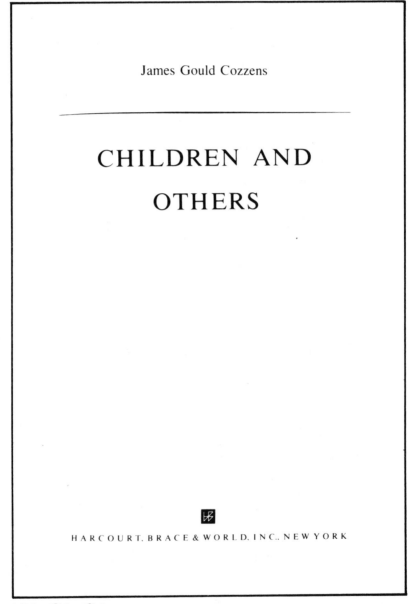

James Gould Cozzens

CHILDREN AND
OTHERS

HARCOURT, BRACE & WORLD, INC., NEW YORK

A 17.1.a: 8⁵⁄₁₆″ × 5⁹⁄₁₆″

[i–viii] [1–2] 3–104 [105–106] 107–192 [193–194] 195–232 [233–234] 235–298 [299–300] 301–343 [344]

$[1–11]^{16}$

Contents: p. i: half title; p. ii: blank; p. iii: 'Books by James Gould Cozzens' *[SSSP, LA, Castaway, M&B, AMT, J&U, GOH, BLP, C&O]*; p. iv: blank; p. v: title; p. vi: copyright; pp. vii–viii: contents; p. 1: 'PART ONE | [tapered rule] | CHILD'S PLAY'; p. 2: blank; pp. 3–343: text, headed 'King Midas Has Ass's Ears'; p. 344: blank.

17 short stories: "King Midas Has Ass's Ears;"* "Child's Play," "Whose Broad Stripes and Bright Stars," "The Animals' Fair," "Total Stranger," "Something about a Dollar," "Someday You'll Be Sorry," "We'll Recall It with Affection," "The Guns of the Enemy," "*Candida* by Bernard Shaw," "Men Running," "One Hundred Ladies," "My Love to Marcia," "The Way to Go Home," "Every Day's a Holiday," "Farewell to Cuba," "Eyes to See."* Asterisks follow previously unpublished stories.

Typography and paper: 6¼" (6⅝") × 4". 35 lines per page. Running heads: rectos, section titles; versos, story titles. Wove paper.

Binding: Medium blue (#182) V cloth (smooth). Spine goldstamped: '[tapered rule] | JAMES | GOULD | COZZENS | [tapered rule] | Children | and | Others | [tapered rule] | Harcourt, | Brace & World | [boxed HBW logo]'. Medium yellow endpapers. All edges trimmed. Top edge stained light blue.

Dust jacket: Front and spine medium yellow. Front: '[title in blue and red on alphabet blocks] CHILDREN | & | OTHERS | [black] *Stories by* | James Gould Cozzens'. Spine: 'Children | [on alphabet block in red] & | [black] Others | James | Gould | Cozzens | [boxed HBW device] | Harcourt, Brace | & World'. Back: '[in blue and black on white] Books by | James Gould Cozzens | [9 titles]'. Front flap: blurb for *C&O*. Back flap: note on Cozzens.

Publication: 40,000 copies of first printing. Published 29 July 1964. $5.95. Copyright #A 712033.

Printing: Printed by Murray Printing, Forge Village, Mass. Bound by Colonial Press, Clinton, Mass.

Locations: Lilly (dj); MJB (dj). LC deposit copy missing.

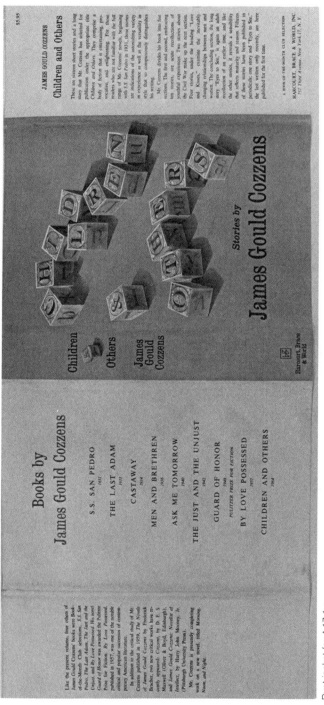

Dust jacket for A 17.1.a

Review copy: Galley proof in white comb binding. Deep reddish orange (#36) paper covers with black HBW pattern; white label on front cover: '[printed] Advance Uncorrected Proofs | [rule] | TITLE | [typed] CHILDREN AND OTHERS | [printed] [rule] | AUTHOR | [typed] James Gould Cozzens | [printed] [rule] | PROBABLE PUBLICATION DATE | [typed] July 29, 1964 | [printed] PROBABLE PRICE | [typed] $5.95 | [printed rule] | [typed] A Book-of-the-Month Club Selection | [printed] Harcourt, Brace & World, Inc. | 757 THIRD AVENUE, NEW YORK, N. Y. 10017'. *Location:* MJB.

A 17.1.b
Book-of-the-Month Club reprint: New York: Harcourt, Brace & World, [1964].

Copyright page: 'First edition' slug removed.

August 1964 BOMC selection. Blindstamped square or dot at lower right on back cover. Dust jacket replaces price on front flap with BOMC notice. Jacket spine adds '0031'.

17.1.c
First edition, first English printing [1965]

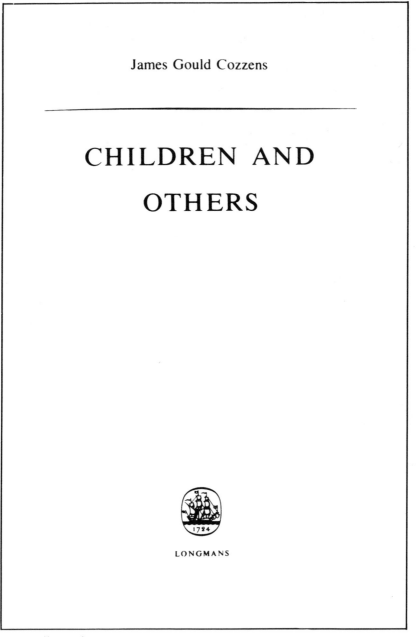

James Gould Cozzens

CHILDREN AND

OTHERS

LONGMANS

A 17.1.c: 7¹¹⁄₁₆″ × 5¹⁄₁₆″

Same pagination as HBW printing.

[1] 2–11^{16}

Contents: Same as HBW printing, except ad for *C&O* on p. i is deleted.

Typography and paper: 6⅛" (6½") × 3¾". 35 lines per page. Wove paper.

Binding: Light greenish gray (#154) paper-covered boards. Spine goldstamped: 'Children | and | Others | * | JAMES | GOULD | COZZENS | *Longmans*'. White wove endpapers. All edges trimmed.

Dust jacket: Front, back, and spine grayish yellow. Front: '[title on white and gray alphabet blocks with red and dark gray letters] CHILDREN | & | OTHERS | [black] *Stories by* | James Gould Cozzens'. Spine: 'Children | [in red on alphabet block] & | [black] Others | James | Gould | Cozzens | LONGMANS'. Back: '[in black and red] OTHER | AVAILABLE BOOKS BY | James Gould Cozzens [6 titles]'. Front flap: blurb for *C&O* in red and black. Back flap: 'Printed in Great Britain LD'.

Publication: Unknown number of copies of the first English printing. Published 5 April 1965. 21s. The A. M. Heath records indicate that 2,964 copies were sold.

Printing: See copyright page.

Locations: BL (2 APR 65); MJB (dj).

A 17.2
Second edition: Greenwich, Conn.: Fawcett, [1968].

Crest #t934. 75¢. Wrappers.

A 17.3
Third edition

James Gould Cozzens | CHILDREN AND OTHERS | Edited with Notes | by | Kinichi Fukuma | and | Kenji Noguchi | THE SIGN OF [boxed device] A GOOD BOOK | THE EIHŌSHA LTD. | —Tokyo—

1968. 290 yen. Wrappers.

3 stories: "King Midas Has Ass's Ears," "The Animals' Fair," "Farewell to Cuba."

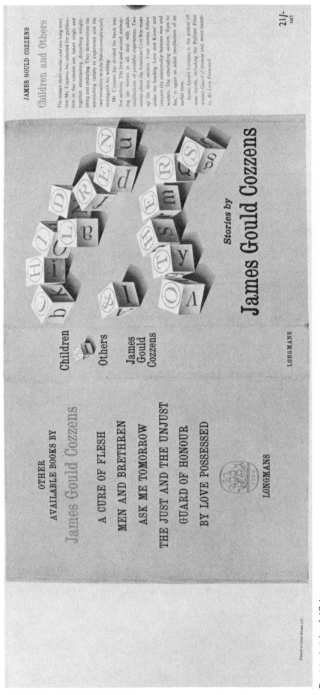

Dust jacket for A.17.1.c

A 18.1.a
First edition, first printing [1968]

JAMES GOULD COZZENS

Morning Noon and Night

They that haue powre to hurt, and will doe none,
That doe not do the thing, they moſt do ſhowe,
Who mouing others, are themſelues as ſtone,
Vnmooued, could, and to temptation flow:
They rightly do inherrit heauens graces,
And husband natures ritches from expence,
They are the Lords and owners of their faces,
Others, but ſtewards of their excellence:

HARCOURT, BRACE & WORLD, INC., NEW YORK

A 18.1.a: 7¹⁵⁄₁₆″ × 5¼″

[i–vi] [1–2] 3–408 [409–410]

[1–13]¹⁶

Contents: p. i: half title; p. ii: blank; p. iii: *'Books by James Gould Cozzens' [SSSP, LA, Castaway, M&B, AMT, J&U, GOH, BLP, C&O, MNN];* p. iv: blank; p. v: title; p. vi: copyright; p. 1: half title; p. 2: blank; pp. 3–408: text, headed 'ONE'; pp. 409–410: blank.

Typography and paper: 6" (6¼") × 3⅝". 32 lines per page. No running heads. Wove paper.

Binding: Goldstamped dark grayish brown (#62) V cloth (smooth). Front: '[gothic] Cozzens'. Spine: '[vertical] COZZENS | [7 thick and thin rules] | Morning Noon | and Night | [horizontal] UNIFORM | EDITION | [boxed HBW logo] | *Harcourt, | Brace & | World'.* Brownish orange endpapers. All edges trimmed. Top edge stained light brown.

Dust jacket: Printed on white. Front: '[gray shaded in orange] Morning | [gray shaded in yellow] Noon | [gray shaded in blue] and Night | [black] JAMES GOULD | COZZENS'. Spine: '[gray shaded in orange] Morning | [gray shaded in yellow] Noon | [gray shaded in blue] and Night | [black] JAMES GOULD | COZZENS | [boxed HBJ logo] | HARCOURT, BRACE & | WORLD'. Back: 'Books by James Gould Cozzens [10 titles]'. Front flap: blurb for *MNN.* Back flap: photo of Cozzens by Slim Aarons with biographical note and plan for uniform edition: 'With the publication of *Morning Noon and Night,* | Harcourt, Brace & World continues a program that | will ultimately make available all books by James | Gould Cozzens in a uniform edition. Each volume is | set in Baskerville and bound in a brown linen finish, | with a brown topstain and gold end papers. Two | other titles are now available in this format: *S.S. San* | *Pedro* and *Castaway.* If you would like to receive, | without cost, a uniform-edition jacket for your copy | of *Morning Noon and Night,* please write to the Trade | Promotion Department, Harcourt, Brace & World, | 757 Third Avenue, New York, N.Y. 10017.'

Uniform Edition dust jacket: Front and spine printed on black. Front: '[white] JAMES | GOULD | COZZENS | [white on blue panel] UNIFORM EDITION | [orange panel] | [black on white panel] Morning | Noon | and Night'. Spine: '[vertically, white] James Gould Cozzens | UNIFORM EDITION | [blue panel] | [orange panel] | black on white panel] [vertically] Morning Noon | and Night | [horizontally] [boxed HBW logo] | Harcourt, | Brace & | World'. Back: same as first-printing jacket, but omits name of designer. Front flap: same as first-printing jacket. Back flap replaces Uniform Edition note with new note and adds name of designer.

Dust jacket for A18.1.a

Publication: 100,000 copies of the first printing. Published 26 August 1968. $5.95. Copyright #A 15918.

Printing: Printed and bound by Colonial Press, Clinton, Mass.

Locations: LC (SEP-3 1968); MJB (both djs).

Review copy: Page proof perfect bound in deep reddish orange (#36) wrappers with black HBW pattern; white label on front cover: '[printed in black] Advance Uncorrected Proofs | [rule] | TITLE | [typed in black] MORNING NOON AND NIGHT | [printed] [rule] | AUTHOR | [typed] James Gould Cozzens | [printed] [rule] | PROBABLE PUBLICATION DATE | PROBABLE PRICE | [rule] | Harcourt, Brace & World, Inc. | 757 THIRD AVENUE, NEW YORK, N. Y. 10017'. *Location:* MJB.

A 18.1.b
Book-of-the-Month Club printings: New York: Harcourt, Brace & World. [1968].

Copyright page: 'FIRST EDITION' slug retained.

August 1968 BOMC selection. Blindstamped square at lower right on back cover; 'UNIFORM EDITION' removed from spine. Dust jacket replaces price on front flap with BOMC notice. Jacket spine adds '1075'. A BOMC printing also appeared with 'FIRST EDITION' slug replaced by 'W'.

Dust jacket for Uniform Edition of A 18.1.a

A 18.1.c
First edition, English printing [1969]

JAMES GOULD COZZENS

Morning Noon and Night

They that haue powre to hurt, and will doe none,
That doe not do the thing, they moſt do ſhowe,
Who mouing others, are themſelues as ſtone,
Vnmooued, could, and to temptation flow:
They rightly do inherrit heauens graces,
And husband natures ritches from expence,
They are the Lords and owners of their faces,
Others, but ſtewards of their excellence:

LONGMANS

A 18.1.c: 8″ × 5³⁄₁₆″

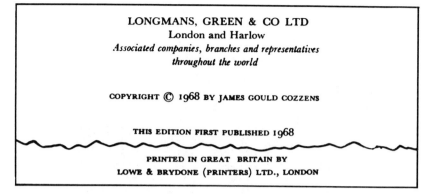

Same pagination as HBW printing.

[A] B–I K–N¹⁶

Contents: Same as HBW printing.

Typography and paper: 6¹⁄₁₆″ (6⁵⁄₁₆″) × 3⅝″. 32 lines per page. No running heads. Wove paper.

Binding: Brilliant greenish blue (#168) paper-covered boards. Spine goldstamped: 'Morning | Noon | and | Night | [2 rules] | James | Gould | Cozzens | Longmans'. White wove endpapers. All edges trimmed.

Dust jacket: Front and spine have white, red, greenish blue, and dark blue panels. Front: '[dark blue on white panel] Morning | Noon and Night | [white on dark blue panel] James | Gould | Cozzens | Author of By Love Possessed'. Spine: '[dark blue on white panel] Morning | Noon | and | Night | [white on dark blue panel] James | Gould | Cozzens | Longmans'. Back: photo of Cozzens by Slim Aarons with biographical note. Front and back flaps printed in greenish blue and black. Front flap: blurb for *MNN*. Back flap lists 6 books by Cozzens.

Publication: Unknown number of copies of the first English printing. Published 27 January 1969. 30s. The A. M. Heath records indicate that 5,329 copies were sold.

Printing: See copyright page.

Locations: BL (19 DEC 68); Lilly (dj); MJB (dj).

Collation: No textual alterations have been found in the first English printing of *Morning Noon and Night*.

A 18.1.d

Second English printing: London: Book Club Associates, [1969?].

The A. M. Heath records indicate that 5,899 copies were sold.

A 18.2

Second edition: [New York]: New American Library, [1970].

Signet #Y 4150. $1.25. Wrappers.

Dust jacket for A 18.1.c

A 19 A FLOWER IN HER HAIR

A 19.1
Only edition, only printing (1975)

A 19.1: illustration and author's name in grayish brown; 8^{15}⁄₁₆″ × 5^{15}⁄₁₆″

Copyright page: '[light grayish brown BC logo] | [black] *A Bruccoli Clark Collector's Edition* | [light grayish brown] Copyright © 1974 by James Gould Cozzens | All rights reserved | Printed in the United States of America'.

[1–7] 8–10 [11–12] 13–31 [32]

[1–2]⁸

Contents: p. 1: half title; p. 2: blank; p. 3: certificate of limitation: '[light grayish brown] A BRUCCOLI CLARK COLLECTOR'S EDITION | [black] This collector's edition is limited to | 350 copies, of which 300 are for sale. | This copy is copy number | [number] | And is here signed by the author | [signature]' (copies 301–350 are designated 'NFS'); p. 4: blank; p. 5: title; p. 6: copyright; pp. 7–10: 'FOREWORD'; p. 11: half title; p. 12: blank; pp. 13–32: text.

Typography and paper: 6″ (6⁵⁄₁₆″) × 4⁵⁄₁₆″. 31 lines per page. No running heads. Laid paper with vertical chain lines; watermarked 'Beckett'.

Binding: Dark grayish yellow (#91) V cloth (smooth). Front has dark gray yellowish brown (#81) label, printed in white: '[within double rules frame] A FLOWER IN | HER HAIR | [leaves] | James Gould Cozzens'. Light olive brown (#94) laid endpapers. All edges trimmed.

Publication: 350 numbered copies. Published 10 April 1975. $35. Copyright #A 627531.

Printing: Printed and bound by Williams Printing, Nashville, Tenn.

Locations: LC (APR 18 1975); Lilly; MJB.

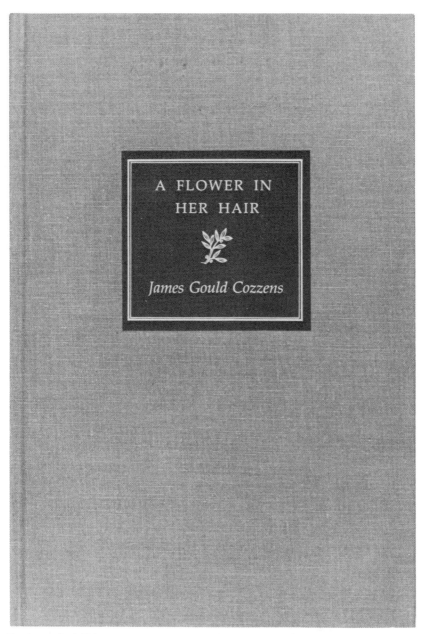

A FLOWER IN
HER HAIR

James Gould Cozzens

Front cover for A 19.1

A 20 A ROPE FOR DR. WEBSTER

A 20.1
Only edition, only printing (1976)

A

Rope for

Dr. Webster

JAMES GOULD COZZENS

BRUCCOLI CLARK

Bloomfield Hills, Michigan &
Columbia, South Carolina
1976

A 20.1: 8⁷⁄₁₆″ × 5⁷⁄₁₆″

Copyright page: 'A Rope for Dr. Webster | Copyright © 1976 | by | James Gould Cozzens'.

[1–4] 5–12 [13–14] 15 [16] 17–19 [20] 21 [22] 23–25 [26] 27 [28] 29 [30] 31 [32]

[1]¹⁶

Contents: p. 1: half title; p. 2: frontispiece; p. 3: title; p. 4: copyright; pp. 5–12: *'Laborious | Explanatory Note';* p. 13: half title; p. 14: blank; p. 15: text; p. 16: illustration; pp. 17–19: text; p. 20: illustration; p. 21: text; p. 22: illustration; pp. 23–25: text; p. 26: illustration; p. 27: text; p. 28: blank; p. 29: text; p. 30: illustration; p. 31: text; p. 32: blank.

Typography and paper: 6⅞" (7¼") × 3¹³⁄₁₆". 31 lines per page. No running heads. Laid yellowish white paper with vertical chain lines; watermarked 'Beckett'. Entire book printed in brown ink. Illustrations by Robert Nance.

Binding: Sheets tied at top through two holes with yellow cord in hinged box with very deep red (#14) plush lid; p. 32 pasted to inside of box bottom. Outside of box lid has gold label: '[within single-rule frame] *A | Rope for | Dr. Webster* | JAMES GOULD COZZENS | [leaf]'. Certificate of limitation pasted to inside of box lid: 'This Is Copy [number] Of A Limited First | Printing Of Three Hundred And Fifty | Signed Copies Of *A Rope for Doctor Web-* | *ster.* Copies Numbered 1 Through 300 Are For Sale; Numbers I Through L Are | Reserved For The Author And Publisher. | [signature] | [rule]'. All edges trimmed.

Publication: Of the 350 numbered copies, 115 were spoiled at the bindery and destroyed. Published 21 August 1976. $35. Copyright #A 773742.

Printing: Printed and bound by Heritage Printers, Charlotte, N.C.

Locations: LC (AUG 30 1976); MJB.

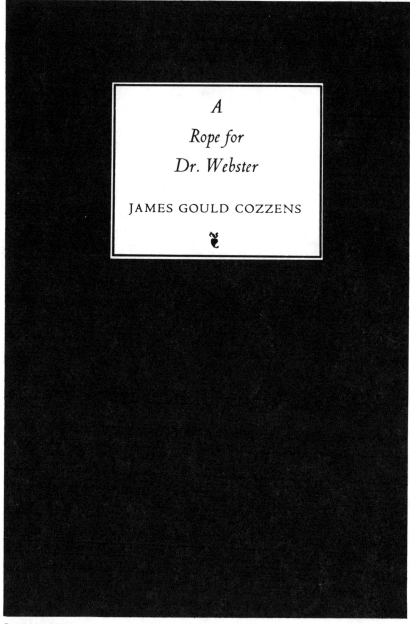

A
Rope for
Dr. Webster

JAMES GOULD COZZENS

Box lid for A 20.1

A 21 SOME PUTATIVE FACTS OF HARD RECORD

A 21.1
Only edition, only printing [1978]

SOME PUTATIVE FACTS
OF HARD RECORD
OR
HE COMMENCES AUTHOUR
AETATIS SUAE 19–20

Excerpts from 1923 MS Diary
and a Few Notes

by James Gould Cozzens

Harcourt Brace Jovanovich
New York and London
and
Southern Illinois University Press
Carbondale and Edwardsville

A 21.1: 8^{15}/₁₆″ × 5½″

Some Putative Facts of Hard Record

Two hundred and fifty copies of this book, which is an excerpt from *Just Representations: A James Gould Cozzens Reader*, published on the occasion of James Gould Cozzens's seventy-fifth birthday, have been printed and bound for friends of the author, of Harcourt Brace Jovanovich, Inc., and of Southern Illinois University Press.

Some Putative Facts of Hard Record has been designed by Richard Neal, composed in Monotype Bembo types, eleven point, and printed on Saint Giles "Blanc," at Heritage Printers, Inc. and bound by William M. Robbins & Sons, Inc.

This is copy number

24

Certificate of limitation for A 21.1

Copyright page: 'Copyright © 1978 by James Gould Cozzens | All rights reserved | Printed in the United States of America'.

[1–6] 7–16

[1]⁸

Contents: p. 1: certificate of limitation; p. 2: blank; p. 3: title; p. 4: copyright; p. 5: half title; p. 6: blank; pp. 7–16: text.

Typography and paper: 6⅛″ (6⁷⁄₁₆″) × 3⅜″. No running heads. Laid paper with vertical chain lines; watermarked: '[helmeted head] | [within double oval frame] HBJ | [hand] | St-Gilles'.

Binding: Dark grayish yellow (#91) V cloth (smooth). Front goldstamped with signature of James Gould Cozzens. Light yellowish brown (#76) endpapers. Top edge trimmed.

Publication: 250 numbered copies; also 30 unnumbered copies. Not for sale. Copies received at Southern Illinois University Press 3 August 1978.

Printing: Composed and printed by Heritage Printers, Charlotte, N.C. Bound by William M. Robbins & Sons, Roachdale, Ind.

Locations: MJB, Southern Illinois University.

AA. Supplement

Books Edited or Revised by Cozzens

AA 1 LANTERNS JUNKS AND JADE
(1926)

LANTERNS | JUNKS AND JADE | BY | SAMUEL MORRILL | [publisher's seal] | NEW YORK | FREDERICK A. STOKES COMPANY | MCMXXVI

Copyright page: 'Copyright, 1926, by | FREDERICK A. STOKES COMPANY | [rule] | *All rights reserved* | *Printed in the United States of America*'.

[i–iv] v–viii 1–287 [288–296]

[1–19]⁸

Cozzens revised or rewrote this travel book. In an 18 February 1927 letter to his mother Cozzens mentioned *Lanterns Junks and Jade* as "once written at such labor by the hard worked self for Samuel Morrill."

Locations: LC; MJB.

AA 2 ZOOM!
(1931)

[within triple-rules frame] ZOOM! | BY | GEORGE R. WHITE | LONGMANS, GREEN AND CO. | NEW YORK • TORONTO | 1931

Copyright page: 'WHITE | ZOOM! | COPYRIGHT • 1931 | BY GEORGE R. WHITE | FIRST EDITION | PRINTED IN THE UNITED STATES OF AMERICA'.

[i–iv] v–vii [viii] ix [x] 1–182

[1–12]⁸

Cozzens revised and edited this aviation primer in 1929.

Locations: LC; Georgia Tech.

AA 3 PACIFIC RELATIONS
(1942)

THE | UNITED STATES | IN A NEW WORLD | *A Series of reports on potential courses* | *for democratic action. Prepared under the* | *auspices of the Editors of Fortune* | [rule] | II: PACIFIC RELATIONS | [rule] | Supplement to FORTUNE, August, 1942 | Copyright, 1942, by TIME INC.

[A–B] [1] 2 [3] 4–5 [6] 7–18 [19] 20–21 [22] 23–25 [26] 27 [28–29] 30–32 [33–34]

[1]¹⁸

Printed wrappers. Cover title. Cozzens rewrote this report by Henry Luce's Postwar Research Committee.

Locations: Time, Inc.; University of South Carolina.

B. First-Appearance Contributions to Books

B 1 KENT SCHOOL YEAR BOOK
1922

[within 2 sets of double-rules frame] [gothic] Kent School | Year Book | 1922 | Edited by the Sixth Form

Kent, Conn., 1922.

"The Class History," pp. 9, 11, 13, 15. Previously unpublished. Unsigned, but Cozzens was the class historian. Reprinted in *Checklist*.

Locations: Kent School; MJB.

B 2 MORROW'S ALMANACK FOR 1929
1928

[within decorated triple-rules frame] MORROW'S | ALMANACK | for the Year of Our Lord | 1929 | [4 lines of type] | [wavy rule] | [8 lines of type] | [wavy rule] | BURTON RASCOE, *Philom.* | [wavy rule] | NEW [WM bird device] YORK | [wavy rule] | *Pub. & sold by* WM. MORROW & CO. removed | from their old offices over Mr. Schwartz's & now located | hard by the old Mad. Sq. Garden site on 4th Ave. Also | *obt'ble* at all bookstores by the gross, doz., or single.

"Breaking the Week in Cuba," pp. 107–113. Previously unpublished.

B 3 MORROW'S ALMANACK FOR 1930
1929

[within decorated triple-rules frame] [decoration] MORROW'S [decoration] | ALMA-NACK | [decoration] AND [decoration] | EVERY-DAY BOOK | FOR 1930 | [wavy rule] | THAYER HOBSON, *Philom.* | [wavy rule] | NEW [WM bird device] YORK | [wavy rule] | *Pub. & sold by* WM. MORROW from their | offices on the 13th floor of the building on the N.W. | corner of 4th Ave. and 27th St. Also *obt'ble* in any | quantity from your bookseller.

"Portrait of a Chief Officer on His Birthday," pp. 220–223. Previously unpublished.

B 4 BALZAC'S MASTERPIECES
1931

[within decorated single-rule frame] *BALZAC'S* | *MASTERPIECES* | *Ten Novels* | By | HONORE DE BALZAC | *with an introduction by* | JAMES GOULD COZZENS | Philadelphia | DAVID McKAY COMPANY | Washington Square | 1931

"Introduction," pp. ix–xii. Previously unpublished. | "A certain now long deceased rare book dealer had undertaken the Balzac compilation for McKay, providing a foreword. This proved to be so illiterate that the publisher's editor asked B & B [Brandt & Brandt literary agency] for help. I agreed to see what I could do (I was paid, I believe, $250). The estimate of Balzac (then and now far from mine) I didn't regard as my business. However, the foreword's 'writer' seeing his work slightly straightened out looked on it as ruined and though he had been paid to produce a publishable piece more or less furiously refused to sign it. Frustrated, feeling he needed a signature, the publisher asked me if I would sign. Since I'd been paid (and perhaps because I never thought anyone would see or read the stuff anyway) I agreed. Older and more experienced I of course wouldn't have; but that was then; and so that to my now confusion, is now definitively that. My simplicity's condign punishment is the fact that today it must be taken as my very own vapid judgment and abominable prose" ("Introduction," in Meriwether, *James Gould Cozzens A Checklist,* p. 1).

B 5 O. HENRY MEMORIAL AWARD PRIZE STORIES OF 1932
1932

O. HENRY | MEMORIAL AWARD | *Prize Stories of 1932* | SELECTED AND EDITED BY | BLANCHE COLTON WILLIAMS | *Author of* "A HANDBOOK ON STORY WRITING" | "OUR SHORT STORY WRITERS," *Etc.* | *Head, Department of English,* | *Hunter College of the* | *City of New York* | [orange DD anchor device] | DOUBLEDAY, DORAN & COMPANY, INC. | GARDEN CITY, NEW YORK | 1932

On copyright page: 'FIRST EDITION'.

"Farewell to Cuba," pp. 19–38. See C 52. This story won second prize.

B 6 O. HENRY MEMORIAL AWARD PRIZE STORIES OF 1936
1936

O. HENRY | MEMORIAL AWARD | *Prize Stories of 1936* | SELECTED AND EDITED BY | HARRY HANSEN | *Literary Editor* | *of the New York World-Telegram* | [DD anchor device] | DOUBLEDAY, DORAN & COMPANY, INC. | GARDEN CITY, NEW YORK | 1936

On copyright page: 'FIRST EDITION'.

"Total Stranger," pp. 1–22. See C 65. This story won first prize.

Note: Prize Stories of 1936 preceded *Post Stories of 1936* (Boston: Little, Brown, 1937)—which also published "Total Stranger."

B 7 STORIES FOR MEN
1936

[within 6-rules frame] Stories | FOR MEN | *An Anthology by* | CHARLES GRAYSON | [Little, Brown device] | BOSTON | LITTLE, BROWN, AND COMPANY | 1936

"Success Story," pp. 159–162. See C 63.

B 8 PENGUIN PARADE 1
1937

PENGUIN PARADE | new stories, poems, etc, by | contemporary writers | 1 | EDITED BY | DENYS KILHAM ROBERTS | [penguin] | PENGUIN BOOKS LIMITED | HARMONDS-WORTH MIDDLESEX ENGLAND

1937.

"Child's Play," pp. 123–143. See C 70.

B 9 PENGUIN PARADE 2
1938

PENGUIN PARADE | new stories, poems, etc, by | contemporary writers | 2 | EDITED BY | DENYS KILHAM ROBERTS | [penguin] | PENGUIN BOOKS LIMITED | HARMONDS-WORTH MIDDLESEX ENGLAND

1938.

"The Animals' Fair," pp. 121–145. See C 69.

B 10 PENGUIN PARADE 5
1939

PENGUIN PARADE | new stories, poems, etc., by | contemporary writers | 5 | EDITED BY | DENYS KILHAM ROBERTS | [penguin] | PENGUIN BOOKS LIMITED | HARMONDS-WORTH MIDDLESEX ENGLAND

1939.

"Son and Heir," pp. 155–176. See C 72.

B 11 CONTEMPORARY AMERICAN AUTHORS
1940

CONTEMPORARY | American Authors | *A Critical Survey and 219 Bio-Bibliographies* | FRED B. MILLETT | *New York* | HARCOURT, BRACE AND COMPANY | 1940

Excerpt from letter, p. 304. Previously unpublished.

B 12 TWENTIETH CENTURY AUTHORS
1942

TWENTIETH CENTURY | AUTHORS | A Biographical Dictionary of Modern Literature | *Edited by* | STANLEY J. KUNITZ | *and* | HOWARD HAYCRAFT | COMPLETE IN ONE VOLUME WITH | 1850 BIOGRAPHIES AND | 1700 PORTRAITS | [circular lighthouse device] | NEW YORK | THE H. W. WILSON COMPANY | NINETEEN HUNDRED FORTY-TWO

Autobiographical notes by Cozzens, p. 323. Previously unpublished.

B 13 UNIFIED ENGLISH COMPOSITION
1942

Unified English Composition | GERALD D. SANDERS | HOOVER H. JORDAN | ROBERT M. LIMPUS | WALLACE H. MAGOON | *Michigan State Normal College* | F. S. CROFTS & CO. NEW YORK | 1942

"Foot in It," pp. 695–697. See C 64.

B 14 THE HARVARD ADVOCATE ANTHOLOGY
1950

The | HARVARD | *ADVOCATE* | Anthology | Edited by Donald Hall | [line of decorations] | *"If one seeks a monument to the little old paper,* | *let him look about in the list of young writers,* | *and see how many of them became famous."* | —W. G. Peckham, '67, in *The Harvard Advocate;* | *Fifty Year Book,* 1916 | [line of decorations] | TWAYNE PUBLISHERS, INC. • NEW YORK

1950.

"Condolence" and "Remember the Rose," pp. 216–223. See C 16, C 22.

B 15 CURRENT BIOGRAPHY 1949
1950

CURRENT BIOGRAPHY | WHO'S NEWS AND WHY | 1949 | EDITED BY | Anna Rothe | [lighthouse device] | THE H. W. WILSON COMPANY | NEW YORK, N.Y.

1950.

Autobiographical notes by Cozzens, pp. 125–126. Previously unpublished.

B 16 STORIES FOR MEN
1953

STORIES FOR MEN | [decorated rule] *The Fourth Round* | An Anthology Edited by | CHARLES GRAYSON | *New York:* HENRY HOLT AND COMPANY

1953.

"Men Running," pp. 201–214. See C 71.

B 17 FATHER SILL'S BIRTHDAY
1956

[Portrait of Father Frederick Herbert Sill] | FATHER SILL'S BIRTHDAY, MARCH 10, 1956 | KENT SCHOOL'S FIFTIETH YEAR

Kent, Conn.: Kent School, 1956

Cover title. Wrappers. Unpaged. Program for the dinner at the Hotel Waldorf-Astoria, New York, 10 March 1956.

"FHS: A Faith that Did Not Fail." Previously unpublished. Reprinted in *Fifty Years 1906– 1956 Kent School* (Kent, Conn.: Committee for Kent School's 50th Anniversary Celebration, 1956). See also B 30.

Locations: Kent School; MJB.

B 18 THE BEST SHORT STORIES OF WORLD WAR II
1957

* * | *THE BEST SHORT STORIES* | *OF WORLD WAR II* | * | AN AMERICAN ANTHOLOGY | * * * | *Edited By* | CHARLES A. FENTON | [Viking device] | *New York* * THE VIKING PRESS * *1957*

Statement on "The Four Freedoms" by Edward Newhouse, p. 297. Previously unpublished.

B 19 COPEY OF HARVARD
1960

Copey of Harvard | *A Biography of Charles Townsend Copeland* | BY J. DONALD ADAMS | WITH ILLUSTRATIONS | [gothic] The Riverside Press Cambridge | [roman] HOUGHTON MIFFLIN COMPANY BOSTON | 1960

Excerpt from letter, pp. 151–152: "When I was at college . . . I had the much mistaken idea that I already knew how to write and did not need Professor Copeland's course, so I never took it." Previously unpublished.

B 20 PROCEEDINGS
1961

PROCEEDINGS | OF THE | AMERICAN ACADEMY | OF ARTS AND LETTERS | AND THE | NATIONAL INSTITUTE | OF ARTS AND LETTERS | [2 medallions] | *SECOND SERIES • NUMBER ELEVEN* | [tapered rule] | NEW YORK • 1961

Wrappers.

"Presentation to James Gould Cozzens of the Howells Medal for Fiction by Malcolm Cowley of the Institute," pp. 38–39. Quotes from Cozzens' letter of acceptance. Previously unpublished.

B 21 STUDIES IN BIBLIOGRAPHY 15
1962

STUDIES IN | BIBLIOGRAPHY | PAPERS OF THE BIBLIOGRAPHICAL SOCIETY | OF THE UNIVERSITY OF VIRGINIA | Edited by | FREDSON BOWERS | [circular U. of Va. seal] | Volume Fifteen | *Charlottesville, Virginia* | Bibliographical Society of the University of Virginia | 1962

James B. Meriwether, "The English Editions of James Gould Cozzens," pp. 207–217. Includes excerpts from 2 Cozzens letters. Previously unpublished.

B 22 ROSES OF YESTERDAY AND TODAY
1963

[within 3 sets of rules frame decorated with roses and ribbons] *Roses of Yesterday* | *and Today* | Old-Rare-Unusual | [rule] | Selected Modern Roses | [rose] | *Will Tillotson's Roses* | Brown's Valley Road | WATSONVILLE, CALIFORNIA | 1963 | [below frame] [initialed drawing of roses and Cupid]

Printed wrappers.

Statement, p. 34; excerpt from letter, p. 42. Previously unpublished.

Location: Princeton.

B 23 CONTEMPORARY AUTHORS 11–12
1965

[script] Contemporary | Authors | [roman] A BIO-BIBLIOGRAPHICAL GUIDE TO | CURRENT AUTHORS AND THEIR WORKS | JAMES M. ETHRIDGE | BARBARA KOPALA | Editors | [script] volumes 11–12 | [roman] *GALE RESEARCH COMPANY • THE BOOK TOWER • DETROIT 26, MICHIGAN*

1965.

Comment on critic, p. 95. Previously unpublished.

B 24 ROSES OF YESTERDAY
1967

Dorothy Stemler and Nanae Ito | *Roses of Yesterday* | 18 Reproductions | of Original Water Colors | With a Foreword | by James Gould Cozzens | [drawing of roses] | Hallmark Cards, Inc. | Kansas City, Missouri

1967.

"Foreword," pp. 5–12; excerpt on back of dust jacket. Previously unpublished.

B 25 STANDARDS
1967

[left] [wavy lines within rectangular frame] [right] NEW EDITION | Standards | CADET HANDBOOK | OF COMPOSITION | DEPARTMENT OF ENGLISH | UNITED STATES AIR FORCE ACADEMY

1967? Cover title. Wrappers.

["Writing Clearly"], pp. 22–23. See C 78.

Locations: U. S. Air Force Academy; Princeton; MJB.

B 26 JAMES GOULD COZZENS   A CHECKLIST
1972

[2-page title] [across both pages] ULD COZZENS JAMES GOULD COZZENS JAMES GOULD COZZENS

JAMES GOULD COZZENS | [left page] [photo of Cozzens] | [right page] A CHECKLIST | Compiled by James B. Meriwether | Introduction | by | James Gould Cozzens | [BC logo] A BRUCCOLI [diamond] CLARK BOOK | PUBLISHED BY GALE RESEARCH, BOOK TOWER, DETROIT

1972.

"Introduction," pp. 1–2; "Preface" to *The Criticisms of John Keats on English Poetry,* plates 2–3 (see A 3); letters to Meriwether, plates 4–6; TS pages of *MNN* draft, plates 7–8; original text of letter to *Fact,* plate 14. Previously unpublished.

B 27 WHO'S WHO 1976–1977
1976

Who's Who | in America ® | 39th edition | 1976–1977 | Volume 1 | MARQUIS | Who's Who | Marquis Who's Who, Inc. | 200 East Ohio Street | Chicago, Illinois 60611 U.S.A.

1976.

Statement, p. 678: "The longer I watch men and life, the surer I get that success whenever more than minor comes of luck alone. By comparison, no principles, ideas, goals and standards of conduct matter much in an achieving of it." Previously unpublished.

Note: Beginning with Volume 17 (1932–1933) Cozzens provided biographical details for *Who's Who in America.* Cozzens also provided biographical details for the following *Harvard Class of 1926 Reports: First Report* (1927), *Decennial Report* (1936), *Quindecennial Report* (1941), *20th Anniversary Report* (1946), *25th Anniversary Report* (1951), *40th Anniversary Report* (1966), *50th Anniversary Report* (1976).

B 28 SAMUEL JOHNSON
1977

W. Jackson Bate, *Samuel Johnson.* New York & London: Harcourt Brace Jovanovich, [1977].

Statement on back of dust jacket. Previously unpublished.

B 29 THE FILMS OF FRANK CAPRA
1977

The Films of | FRANK CAPRA | by Victor Scherle and William Turner Levy | *INTRODUCTION BY THE HON. WILLIAM O. DOUGLAS* | THE CITADEL PRESS   SECAUCUS, N.J.

1977.

Statement, p. 16. Previously unpublished.

B 30 JUST REPRESENTATIONS
1978

[rule] *Just Representations* | A | JAMES GOULD COZZENS | READER | Edited and with an Introduction | by Matthew J. Bruccoli | Southern Illinois University Press | CARBON-

DALE AND EDWARDSVILLE | *and* | Harcourt Brace Jovanovich | NEW YORK AND LONDON

1978.

On copyright page: 'First edition | ABCDEFGHIJ'.

Published simultaneously in a clothbound printing by Southern Illinois University Press and a paperbound Harvest printing by Harcourt Brace Jovanovich.

Novels: *Ask Me Tomorrow* and excerpts from *The Last Adam, Men and Brethren, The Just and The Unjust, Guard of Honor, By Love Possessed, Morning Noon and Night.* Stories: "The Way to Go Home," "Every Day's a Holiday," and "One Hundred Ladies." Articles: "Notes on a Difficulty of Law by One Unlearned in It,"* "The Impact of Intolerable Facts,"* "Foreword" to *Roses of Yesterday,* "FHS: A Faith that Did Not Fail," "Foreword" to *A Flower in Her Hair,* "Laborious Explanatory Note" for *A Rope for Dr. Webster.* Letter to *Fact.* Asterisks follow items that are first book appearances. "Some Putative Facts of Hard Record or He Commences Authour Aetatis Suae 19–20 Excerpts from 1923 MS Diary and a Few Notes," pp. xxiii–xxxii, was previously unpublished. See keepsake, A 21. This collection also includes articles about Cozzens by George Garrett, Jerome Weidman, Noel Perrin, Frederick Bracher, Brendan Gill, and Richard M. Ludwig (see C 87).

Review copies: SIU's clothbound printing: Xeroxed page proofs in a comb binding. HBJ's paperbound printing: Xeroxed page proofs perfect-bound in blue printed wrappers. *Location:* MJB (both).

Special copies: 4 copies bound in full leather with slipcase for James Gould Cozzens, William Jovanovich, Vernon Sternberg, and Matthew J. Bruccoli.

B 31 NEW ACQUIST OF TRUE EXPERIENCE
1979

James Gould | Cozzens | New Acquist of True Experience | [rule] | *Edited by* | Matthew J. Bruccoli | [rule] | Southern Illinois University Press | *Carbondale and Edwardsville* | Feffer & Simons, Inc. | London and Amsterdam

1979.

Previously unpublished excerpts from Cozzens' letters and notebooks, pp. v, xii–xiii, 61, 64, 72.

B 32 STUDIES IN THE AMERICAN RENAISSANCE
1980

[3 rules] | STUDIES | IN THE | AMERICAN | RENAISSANCE | [3 rules] | 1980 | [3 rules] | *Edited by* JOEL MYERSON | Boston: | TWAYNE PUBLISHERS

1980.

"A Friendly Thinker," pp. 37–39. See C 6.

C. First Appearances in Magazines and Newspapers

C 1
"The Andes," *The Quill* (Staten Island Academy), XXX (January 1915), 5.

Poem.

C 2
"Lord Kitchener," *Digby* (Nova Scotia) *Weekly Courier* (16 June 1916), 1.

Poem.

C 3
"A Democratic School," *The Atlantic Monthly*, CXXV (March 1920), 383–384.

Article. Reprinted as "In Defense of Boarding Schools," *Kent Quarterly*, XII (March 1920), 50–52. See A 1.

C 4
"The Contributors' Column," *The Atlantic Monthly*, CXXV (March 1920), 430.

Excerpt from letter about Kent School.

C 5
"The Trail of the Lakes," *Kent Quarterly*, XII (May 1920), 86–91.

Article.

C 6
"A Friendly Thinker," *Kent Quarterly*, XIII (December 1920), 13–14.

Article. See B 32.

C 7
"Good Old Main Street," *Kent Quarterly*, XIII (March 1921), 40–42.

Article.

C 8
"Religion for Beginners: A Nova Scotian Sketch," *Kent Quarterly*, XIV (December 1921), 25–28.

Article.

C 9
Entry cancelled.

C 10
"A Study in the Art of the Novel," *Kent Quarterly*, XIV (July 1922), 77–79.

Prize essay.

C 11
"The Trust in Princes," *Harvard Advocate*, CIX (1 November 1922), 44.

Poem. Reprinted in *Kent Quarterly*, XV (January 1923), 8.

C 12
Review of *The Bright Shawl*, Joseph Hergesheimer, *Harvard Advocate*, CIX (1 December 1922), 85–86.

C 13
"Where Angels Fear to Tread," *Harvard Advocate*, CIX (1 December 1922), 86.

Poem.

C 14
Review of *Don Rodriguez: Chronicles of Shadow Valley*, by Lord Dunsany, *Harvard Advocate*, CIX (1 January 1923), 120–121.

C 15
"The Passing," *Harvard Advocate*, CIX (1 January 1923), 121.

Poem.

C 16
"Condolence," *Harvard Advocate*, CIX (1 February 1923), 151.

Poem. See B14.

C 17
Letter to the editor, *Harvard Crimson* (7 March 1923), 2.

Reply to review of *Eight More Harvard Poets*.

C 18
Review of *Love and Freindship*, by Jane Austen, *Harvard Advocate*, CIX (7 April 1923), 291.

C 19
"Two Arts," *Harvard Advocate*, CIX (1 May 1923), 347.

Poem.

C 20
"The Virginia Rose: A Ballad for Eunice," *Harvard Advocate*, CIX (1 May 1923), 338–339.

Poem.

C 21
"For a Motet by Josquin de Pres," *Harvard Advocate*, CIX (1 June 1923), 404.

Poem.

C 22
"Remember the Rose," *Harvard Advocate*, CIX (1 June 1923), 395–397.

Short story. See B 14.

C 23
"The Long Elusion," *Casements* (Brown University), (July 1923), unpaged.

Poem.

C 24
"ΑΦΡΟΛΙΤΗΚΓΠΡΙΑ," *Kent Quarterly*, XV (July 1923), 91.

Poem.

C 25
"Romanesque," *Kent Quarterly*, XV (July 1923), 85.

Poem.

C 26
"Blue Seas," *Palms*, I (Autumn 1923), 110.

Poem.

C 27
"Hail and Farewell," *Harvard Advocate*, CX (1 October 1923), 13.

Untitled sonnet.

C 28
Review of *The Shepherd's Pipe*, by Arthur Schnitzler, *Dial*, LXXV (December 1923), 608–610.

This review is signed by Cuthbert Wright, but Cozzens claimed it as his own work.

C 29
"Cambridge Boy Produces Novel Winning Praise" [headline unclear], unlocated scrapbook clipping at Princeton, ca. April 1924.

Interview.

C 30
"Harvard Student To Publish Novel," unlocated scrapbook clipping at Princeton, ca. April 1924.

Interview.

C 31
"Abishag," *Linonia*, I (June 1925), 45–53.

Short story.

C 32
"The Point of View," *Kent Quarterly*, XVII (June 1925), 55–59.

Article.

C 33
"Harvard Author Reviews New Work 'The History of Michael Scarlett'," *Daily Princetonian*, XLVI (12 June 1925), 1, 4.

C 34

"A Letter to a Friend," *Pictorial Review*, XXVII (May 1926), 16, 116–117.

Short story.

C 35

"What You Should Know About the Club Library," *Winged Foot* (New York Athletic Club), XXXVIII (September 1927), 29–30.

Article.

C 36

"Notes from the Club Library," *Winged Foot*, XXXVIII (October 1927), 17.

Article.

C 37

"The Library Talk for the Month," *Winged Foot*, XXXVIII (November 1927), 28–29.

Article.

C 38

"Notes from the Club Library," *Winged Foot*, XXXVIII (December 1927), 42.

Article.

C 39

"Notes from the Club Library," *Winged Foot*, XXXIX (January 1928), 20–21.

Article.

C 40

"Foreign Strand," *Paris Comet*, 11, 4 (September 1928), 4 pp.

Short story. Clipping at Princeton.

C 41

Letter to Harry Salpeter, *New York World* (30 September 1928), 10M.

Comment on James Francis Thierry

C 42

"Future Assured," *The Saturday Evening Post*, CCII (2 November 1929), 22–23, 116, 120–121, 124.

Short story.

C 43

"The Defender of Liberties," *Alhambra*, I (January 1930), 14–17, 54–56.

Short story.

C 44

"Lions Are Lower Today," *The Saturday Evening Post*, CCII (15 February 1930), 36, 38, 40, 154, 158.

Short story.

C 45

"Someday You'll Be Sorry," *The Saturday Evening Post,* CCII (21 June 1930), 44, 47, 60, 63–64, 66.

Short story. *C&O.**

C 46

"S.S. 'San Pedro' A Tale of the Sea," *Scribner's Magazine,* LXXXVIII (August 1930), 113–128, 214–228.

Novelette. See A 7.1.

C 47

"October Occupancy," *American Magazine,* CX (October 1930), 56–59, 153–158.

Short story.

C 48

"We'll Recall It with Affection," *The Saturday Evening Post,* CCIII (4 October 1930), 12–13, 149–150, 152–154.

Short story. *C&O.*

C 49

"The Guns of the Enemy," *The Saturday Evening Post,* CCIII (1 November 1930), 12–13, 74, 77–78, 80, 82.

Short story. *CAO.*

C 50

"Fortune and Men's Eyes," *Woman's Home Companion,* LVIII (February 1931), 29–30, 134, 136, 138, 140.

Short story.

C 51

"Thoughts Brought on by 633 Manuscripts," *Bookman,* LXXIII (June 1931), 381–384.

Article.

C 52

"Farewell to Cuba," *Scribner's Magazine,* XC (November 1931), 533–544.

Short story. *C&O.* See B 5.

C 53

"The Way to Go Home," *The Saturday Evening Post,* CCIV (26 December 1931), 12–13, 59–60.

Short story. *C&O.*

C 54

Ruth Hale, "The Author," *Book-of-the-Month Club News* (December 1932), 3.

Interview.

---

*Indicates that the short story is collected in *Children and Others,* 1964 (A 17).

C 55
Letter to the editor, *Waterbury* (Conn.) *Republican* (21 January 1933), 8.

About setting for *LA*.

C 56
Letter to the editor, *New Milford* (Conn.) *Times* (2 February 1933), 4.

About setting for *LA*.

C 57
Letter to the editor, *Colgate Maroon* (14 March 1933), 2.

About model for Dr. Bull in *LA*.

C 58
"Kent, a New School," *Town & Country*, LXXXVIII (1 August 1933), 38–41, 57.

Article.

C 59
"Every Day's a Holiday," *Scribner's Magazine*, XCIV (December 1933), 339–344.

Short story. *C&O*.

C 60
"My Love to Marcia," *Collier's*, XCII (3 March 1934), 16–17, 46–47.

Short story. *C&O*.

C 61
"Love Leaves Town," *American Magazine*, CXVIII (September 1934), 24–27, 119–121.

Short story.

C 62
"Straight Story," *Collier's*, XCIV (17 November 1934), 22.

Short story.

C 63
"Success Story," *Collier's* XCV (20 April 1935), 26.

Short story. See B 7

C 64
"Foot in It," *Redbook*, LXV (August 1935), 28–29.

Short story. See B 13. Reprinted and anthologized as "Clerical Error."

C 65
"Total Stranger," *The Saturday Evening Post*, CCVIII (15 February 1936), 8–9, 96, 98, 100.

Short story. *C&O*. See B 6.

C 66
"Whose Broad Stripes and Bright Stars," *The Saturday Evening Post*, CCVIII (23 May 1936), 16–17, 69, 71.

Short story. *C&O.*

C 67
"Something about a Dollar," *The Saturday Evening Post*, CCIX (15 August 1936), 27–28, 62, 64.

Short story. *C&O.*

C 68
Foreword to *Kent Quarterly*, I (26 November 1936), 3–4.

C 69
"The Animals' Fair," *The Saturday Evening Post*, CCIX (16 January 1937), 18–19, 47, 50, 53–54.

Short story. *C&O.* See B 9.

C 70
"Child's Play," *The Saturday Evening Post*, CCIX (13 February 1937), 16–17, 61, 63, 65.

Short story. *C&O.* See B 8.

C 71
"Men Running," *The Atlantic Monthly*, CLX (July 1937), 81–91.

Short story. *C&O.* See B 16.

C 72
"Son and Heir," *The Saturday Evening Post*, CCX (2 April 1938), 10–11, 86, 88–89, 91.

Short story. See B 10.

C 73
"The Fuller Brush Co.," *Fortune*, XVIII (October 1938), 69–72, 100, 102, 104.

Article. Between March and December 1938 Cozzens was listed as an editor or associate editor for *Fortune*. Most of his articles were altered by editorial hands, but this unsigned article appeared very much as he had written it. Other articles that Cozzens worked on were "Big Navy" (March 1938), "Oskaloosa vs. the United States" (April 1938), "9,000 Billion Horsepower of Solar Energy" (November 1938), and "You Don't Need to Sue" (December 1938).

C 74
Robert Van Gelder, "James Gould Cozzens at Work," *New York Times Book Review* (23 June 1940), 14.

Interview.

C 75
"Writer Visits Court Here For Atmosphere," *Doylestown* (Pa.) *Intelligencer* (2 July 1940), 1.

Quotes Cozzens.

C 75 A
The Just and the Unjust," *Omnibook*, IV (October 1942), 91–118.

Abridgment.

C 76
"What They're Reading," *Air Force*, XXVI (June 1943), 28.

Article

C 77
"The First Manual," *AFTAD Liaison Bulletin*, no. 41 (29 June 1943), 3.

Article.

Location: Princeton.

C 78
"Writing Clearly," *AFTAD Liaison Bulletin*, no. 45 (9 July 1943), 4.

Article. See B 25.

Location: Princeton.

C 79
"Airways Flying," *Air Transport*, I (September 1943), 39–42.

Article by Cozzens and Bert Moore. See A 14.

C 80
"The Air Force Training Program," *Fortune*, XXIX (February 1944), 147–152, 174, 176, 178, 180, 183–184, 186, 189–190, 193–194.

Unsigned, but headnote credits Cozzens: "In preparing the report that begins on the following page, *Fortune* had the collaboration of a former associate editor, Captain James Gould Cozzens, the novelist." This article was drafted by William Vogel and revised by Cozzens.

C 81
"Cozzens Was Gardening When Word Came Of Pulitzer Prize," *Trenton Evening Times* (6 May 1949), 2.

Interview.

C 82
Review of *The Eagle in the Egg*, by Oliver La Farge, *New York Times Book Review* (24 July 1949), 1, 17.

Reprinted in *Just Representations* (B 30) as "The Impact of Intolerable Facts."

C 83
Ann Biester, "J. G. Cozzens, Pulitzer Author, Grants Interview To Reporter," *Doylestown High School News* (17 March 1950), 2.

C 84
"Notes on a Difficulty of Law by One Unlearned in It," *Bucks County Law Reporter* (Doylestown, Pa.), I (15 November 1951), 3–7.

This article was subsequently circulated in copies made by a mimeograph process. See also B 30.

C 85
Letter to the editor, *New Hope* (Pa.) *Gazette* (15 September 1955), 4.

Opposes election of John W. Eckelberry to the Bucks County bench.

C 86
William DuBois, "In And Out of Books," *New York Times Book Review* (25 August 1957), 8.

Replies to questions.

C 87
Richard M. Ludwig, "A Reading of the James Gould Cozzens Manuscripts," *The Princeton University Library Chronicle*, XIX (Autumn 1957), 1–14.

Quotes from Cozzens' letters; facsimiles TS draft pages for *BLP*. See B 30.

C 88
"The Hermit of Lambertville," *Time*, CXX (2 September 1957), 72–74, 76–77.

Based on interviews.

C 89
"Carl Brandt Dies; A Literary Agent," *New York Times* (14 October 1957), 27.

Quotes Cozzens.

C 90
Review of *Reflections on Hanging,* by Arthur Koestler, *Harvard Law Review*, LXXI (May 1958), 1377–1381.

Note: The book-review section of this issue of the *Harvard Law Review* was distributed as an offprint in gray-green paper covers with the front printed in black.

C 91
"J. G. Cozzens '22 Pulitzer Prize Winner, Prefers The Quiet Life To Plaudits," *The Kent News* (7 May 1959), 2.

Quotes Cozzens.

C 92
Lewis Nichols, "In And Out of Books," *New York Times Book Review* (9 August 1959), 8.

Includes brief statement by Cozzens.

C 93
Letter to the editor, *University: A Princeton Magazine*, I (Fall 1960), 2.

Comments on the magazine.

C 94
Booklist, *The Christian Century*, LXXIX (22 August 1962), 1009.

Reply to the question, "What books did most to shape your vocational attitude and your philosophy of life?" Cozzens provided this list:

Several of the Oz books of Frank Baum
The Motor Boys series, by Clarence Young
Many of the books of G. A. Henty
Jungle Books, by Rudyard Kipling
Swiss Family Robinson, by Johann Wyss
The Lays of Ancient Rome, by Thomas B. Macaulay

C 95
Letter to the editor, *Harvard Alumni Bulletin*, LXV (4 May 1963), 593.

On Harvard architecture.

C 96
Letter, *TV Guide*, XI (24 August 1963), 6–7.

Reply to questions about television preferences.

C 97
Letter to the editor, *The Living Church*, CXLVII (27 October 1963), 17.

On evacuating churches during bomb threats.

C 98
Letter to the editor, *Forbes*, LXXXXII (15 November 1963), 6.

About unsatisfactory American razor blades.

C 99
Letter to *Fact*, I (January–February 1964), 5.

About inaccuracies in *Time* cover story on Cozzens. The text of this letter was rewritten by *Fact*. Cozzens' original letter is published in B 26 and B 30.

C 100
Letter to the editor, *The Living Church*, CXLVIII (22 March 1964), 5.

About distribution of *The Book of Common Prayer*.

C 101
"One Hundred Ladies," *The Saturday Evening Post*, CCXXXVII (11 July 1964), 40, 42–43, 45–47.

Short story. *C&O*.

C 102
"*Candida* by Bernard Shaw," *The Saturday Evening Post*, CCXXXVII (25 July 1964), 50, 52, 54, 57.

Short story. *C&O*.

C 103
Letter to the editor, *Bulletin* (Harvard Club of New York) (April 1965).

Comment on a recipe.

C 104
Letter to the editor, *Harvard Alumni Bulletin*, LXVIII (13 May 1967), 2–3.

Reply to letter by Henry J. Friendly (11 March 1967) about Jewish quota at Harvard.

C 105
Letter to the editor, *Berkshire* (Pittsfield, Mass.) *Eagle* (13 July 1967), p. 13.

Defense of Gen. Charles Lee.

C 106
Letter, *Harvard Class of 1926 Newsletter* (June 1977), 2.

"Going on 74, this '26er hasn't a thing to complain of: and from all I hear and watch, if that ain't News in God's name what would be?"

C 107
Morris H. Wolff, "The Legal Background of Cozzens' *The Just and the Unjust*," *Journal of Modern Literature*, VII (September 1979), 508.

Facsimile of inscription to Edward G. Biester in dedication copy of *J&U*.

CC. Supplement

Unsigned Contributions to the *Kent School News* and the *Kent Quarterly*

Cozzens was on the staff of the *Kent School News* from 1919 to 1922; there were no bylines. He was editor of the *Kent Quarterly* for the December 1921, March 1922, May 1922, and July 1922 issues, and probably wrote most of the editorials. The items in this section have been attributed to Cozzens on the basis of his diary entries.

CC 1
"Suggestions For Library," *Kent School News* (9 April 1920), 4.

Article.

CC 2
Untitled editorial on the ordination of Utey Berkley, *Kent School News* (21 May 1920), 2.

CC 3
"Mr. Hackett Speaks," *Kent School News* (28 May 1920), 1, 4.

Article.

CC 4
Unidentified editorial, *Kent School News* (28 May 1920), 2.

Possibly on Mr. Hackett.

CC 5
Two unidentified editorials, *Kent School News* (10 June 1920), 2.

CC 6
Unidentified editorial, *Kent School News* (10 October 1920).

Issue not seen.

CC 7
Untitled editorial on grades, *Kent School News* (19 November 1920), 2.

CC 8
"Headmaster of Exeter Visits Kent Friday," *Kent School News* (25 November 1920), 1, 3.

Article.

CC 9
"The Speeches," *Kent School News* (3 December 1920), 2.

Article.

CC 10
"The Autumn Issue of Quarterly Out Soon," *Kent School News* (10 December 1920), 1, 3.

Article.

CC 11
Unidentified editorial, *Kent Quarterly*, XIII (December 1920).

Possibly "Books and People," 2.

CC 12
"Mid Winter Dance is Held on Saturday Evening," *Kent School News* (11 February 1921), 1.

Article.

CC 13
"Interesting Program Presented on Saturday Night," *Kent School News* (19 February 1921), 1, 4.

Article.

CC 14
Unidentified editorial, *Kent School News* (25 February 1921), 2.

CC 15
"Last Fourth Formers Speak on Saturday Night," *Kent School News* (4 March 1921), 4.

Article.

CC 16
Untitled editorial on speeches, *Kent School News* (11 March 1921), 2.

CC 17
Unidentified editorial, *Kent Quarterly*, XIII (March 1921).

Possibly "A Plea for Action," 30–31.

CC 18
"Fr. Nichols Stays at School Over Sunday," *Kent School News* (15 April 1921), 1, 3.

Article.

CC 19
"Members of Third Form Speak at School Meeting," *Kent School News* (15 April 1921), 1, 4.

Article.

CC 20
Untitled editorial on Father Nichols, *Kent School News* (15 April 1921), 2.

CC 21
"Brilliant Speeches by Sixth Form at School Meeting," *Kent School News* (29 April 1921), 1–2.

Article.

CC 22
"Death of George H. Bartlett Saddens School," *Kent School News* (13 May 1921), 1, 4.

Article: "doctored beyond recognition by Mr. Schiedt."

CC 23
"Excellent Speeches Rendered by Sixth Formers," *Kent School News* (20 May 1921), 1, 4.

Article.

CC 24
"Speeches by Sixth Formers," *Kent School News* (27 May 1921), 2.

Article.

CC 25
"Mr. Bartlett," *Kent Quarterly*, XIII (May 1921), 57–58.

Editorial—probably by Cozzens.

CC 26
"Napoleon," *Kent Quarterly*, XIII (May 1921), 59–60.

Editorial.

CC 27
"Speeches Present Unusually Good Entertainment," *Kent School News* (7 October 1921), 2–3.

Article.

CC 28
"Saturday Night Speeches are Encouraging," *Kent School News* (14 October 1921), 1, 4.

Article.

CC 29
Untitled editorial on the Pawling game, *Kent School News* (21 October 1921), 2.

CC 30
Untitled editorial on dramatics, *Kent School News* (20 January 1922), 2.

CC 31
Unidentified editorial, *Kent School News* (10 February 1922), 2.

CC 32
Untitled editorial on coal, *Kent School News* (21 April 1922), 2.

CC 33
"Adventuring in Contentment," *Kent Quarterly*, XIV (July 1922), 69–70.

Editorials.

D. Material Quoted in Catalogues

D1
The Brick Row Book Shop . . . Austin, Texas . . . [Catalogue 72; 1961]

#230: Facsimiles inscription in *Confusion:* 'With the Best Wishes of the Author James James Gould Cozzens 1924'.

D2
JOSEPH THE PROVIDER . . . Santa Barbara, California . . . [Catalogue 13; 1974]

#354: Quotes inscription in *Confusion:* 'I began this in the Fall of 1922 and worked very hard at it during the summer of 1923. Robert Hillyer had introduced me to William Stanley Braithwaite who was trying to run a publishing company in Boston. Needless to say he soon failed.'

#355: Quotes inscription in *CP:* 'The physical descriptions here apply pretty accurately to Central Tuinucu in Santa Clara Province. Zacarial was meant to be Sancti Spiritus. I think everything else is a little exaggerated.'

#356: Quotes inscription in *LA:* 'This setting is imagined to be Kent, Connecticut, with a green like New Milford's along US1 as it passes through Kent.'

#357: Quotes inscription in *M&B:* 'The parish of Holy Innocents is imagined to be a combination of St. Bartholomew's and St. Thomas's, with its finances modeled on those of Grace Church in New York City.'

D3
CATALOG 123 . . . AMERICAN LITERATURE . . . HERITAGE BOOKSHOP INC. . . . HOLLYWOOD, CALIFORNIA . . . [1974]

#139: Quotes inscription in *Confusion:* 'The poet, my friend Robert Hillyer, an English instructor at Harvard when this book was published, wrote in a kind review that the most remarkable thing about it was that his 19-year old brother had stuck to it until he read 400 pages, a whole book. I think he was right. 17 July 1960. Shadowbrook, Williamstown, Massachusetts.'

#143: Quotes inscription in *MS:* 'One's only young once, thank goodness. James Gould Cozzens. 6 February 1967, Williamstown, Massachusetts.'

D4
[Joseph the Provider] LITERATURE Modern First Editions Catalogue FOURTEEN [1975]

#201: Repeats items from Catalogue 13 (D2).

#202: Quotes from 2 TLS to an *Esquire* editor: (1) 'I gather you didn't know it, but I'm afraid you were risking your job. You should have checked with Mrs. Parker and Mr. Macdonald. The one and then the other long ago decreed me a dangerous anti-

Semite. . . . Both gnash their teeth and chatter with rage at the drop of my name.' (2) 'I must apologize for having made you go to the trouble of so sober and civil an answer. I wasn't serious about your job; nor even about the metamorphosis into MacCult. You can be absolutely sure some pretty venomous abuse will come from somewhere [after a writer has achieved success]; and you'd better prepare to take it like a man.'

D 5

RARE BOOK & MANUSCRIPT AUCTION & SALE sponsored by THE FRIENDS OF THE DETROIT PUBLIC LIBRARY . . . October 28, 1977 . . .

#16: TS drafts for unfinished novel, "A Skyborn Music"; also quotes letter: 'These are tentative starts dated, I think, 1962. Use was made of a fourth or maybe fifth, start to form the short story *Eyes to See* appearing in *Children and Others* 1964—in short, my planned novel's theme beat me and I saw I'd better abandon it. I don't know how these fragments came to be filed away instead of thrown away. I offer them as evidence that the writer's lot is often not a happy one.'

D 6

HERITAGE BOOKSHOP . . . LOS ANGELES, CALIFORNIA . . . [1979]

Cozzens list, *#8:* Quotes inscription in *J&U:* 'For Webster S. Achey in grateful acknowledgement & some well-considered kidding, sound legal advice and access to the Wiley-Farrell file. Best regards James Gould Cozzens Lambertville, New Jersey 1 July 1942.' With 19 August 1941 TLS.

D 7

[Joseph the Provider] Supplementary List J [1979]

#141: A Rope for Dr. Webster, inscribed: 'No, I never do autographed editions—well, only *little* ones.'

D 8

[Joseph the Provider] MODERN LITERATURE *SUPPLEMENTARY LIST M* [1979]

#279: Typed card, signed: '*Nocturne* may have been "stronger" but the touch here's just as good.' Describes recent reading as 'six or more short gaggings over new contemporary crap.'

E. Translations of Books

BY LOVE POSSESSED

E 1
AŞK HÜKMEDINCE, trans. Gönül Suveren. Istanbul: Türkiye Yayineri, 1958.*

E 2
BESATT AV KÄRLEK, trans. Torsten Blomkvist. Stockholm: Bonniers, 1958.

E 3
BESATT AV KJÆRLIGHET, trans. Peter Magnus. Oslo: Gyldendal, 1958.

E 4
DOOR LIEFDE BEZETEN, trans. Clara Eggink. Amsterdam: Nieuwe Wieken, 1958.

E 5
BESAT AF KÆRLIGHED, trans. Soffy Topsøe. Copenhagen: Thorkild Beck, 1959.

E 6
OSSESSIONE AMOROSA, trans. Adele Cortese Rossi. Milan: Mondadori, 1959.

E 7
VON LIEBE BEHERRSCHT, trans. Trude Rau-Tilling. Frankfurt am Main: S. Fischer, 1959; Bergisch Gladbach: Bastei-Verlag Lübbe, 1970.

E 8
O AMOR TUDO VENCE, trans. Luís Carlos Branco. São Paulo: Instituição Brasileira de Difusão Cultura, 1960.

E 9
PAR L'AMOUR POSSÉDÉ, trans. Marie Tadié. Paris: A. Michel, 1960; Paris: Ambassade du livre, 1961.*

E 10
POSEIDOS POR EL AMOR, trans. Baldomero Porta. Buenos Aires: Goyanarte, 1961.

E 11
V OBLASTI LJUBEZNI, trans. Mira Miheličeva. Ljubljana, Yugoslavia: Cankarjeva založba, 1961.

In Slovene.

E 12
HA-ŠEVUYIM LA-AHAVA, trans. G. Yisreeli. Tel Aviv: Raviv, 1964.*

*Asterisked entries have not been examined by the compiler.

177

CASTAWAY

E 13
IL NAUFRAGO, trans. Tilde Arcelli. Milan: Feltrinelli, 1960.

CHILDREN AND OTHERS

E 14
KINDER UND ANDERE LEUTE, trans. Inge Lindt. Gütersloh, W. Germany: S. Mohn, 1966.

E 15
OS MELHORES CONTOS DE JAMES GOULD COZZENS, trans. Péricles Eugênio da Silva Ramos. São Paulo: Cultrix, 1966.

E 16
JUEGOS DE NIÑOS, trans. Antonio Garza y Garza. Mexico City: Novaro, 1967.

E 17
OJOS PARA VER, trans. Antonio Garza y Garza. Mexico City: Novaro, 1967.

E 18
SHAISHAV ANE BIJU VATO, trans. Harindra Dave. Ahemdabad: Ravani Prakashan Griha, 1968.

In Gujarati.

E 19
BAALPAN, SHAALA ANI JAG, trans. Shamrao N. Oke. Bombay: G. P. Parchure Prakashan Mandir, 1969.

In Marathi.

E 20
BATSHON KA SANSAAR, trans. Krishna Rand Dube. New Delhi: S. R. Suneja Publications, n.d.

In Hindi.

GUARD OF HONOR

E 21
HARAS AL-SHARAF, trans. 'Abd Al-Rahmān Sālih. Al-Qāhirah, United Arab Republic: Al-Dār Al-Misrīyah, 1966.*

THE JUST AND THE UNJUST

E 22
DIE GERECHTEN UND DIE UNGERECHTEN, trans. Georg Goyert. Wiesbaden: Limes, 1946; Wien: Brücken, 1947.

E 23
[The Just and The Unjust]. Athens: Ikaros, 1954.

E 24
LO JUSTO Y LO INJUSTO, trans. Floreal Mazía. Buenos Aires: Hermes, 1956.*

E 25
VOSTRO ONORE, MI OPPONGO, trans. Amalie D'Agostino Schanzer. Milan: Rizzoli, 1963.

E 26
KYAUK CHAUNG LAN PYAN PAY HMU GYI, trans. Yangon Hla Thein. Rangoon, Burma: U Maung Maung Sarpay, 1970.

THE LAST ADAM

E 27
EL ULTIMO ADAN, trans. Manuel Barberá. Buenos Aires, Barcelona & Mexico City: Plaza & Janes, 1964.

MEN AND BRETHREN

E 28
HOMMES ET FRÈRES, trans. Gabrielle Gomel. Paris: Julliard, 1946.*

S.S. SAN PEDRO

E 29
S.S. SAN PEDRO, trans. Yge Foppema. Alkmaar: Schuyt, 1932.*

E 30
EIN SCHIFF GEHT UNTER, trans. Annie Polzer. Berlin: Zsolnay, 1933.*

E 31
S.S. SAN PEDRO, trans. Knute Stuggendorff. Stockholm: Bonniers, 1934.*

E 32
LE SAN PEDRO, trans. Dominique Drouin. Paris: Gallimard, 1950.

E 33
Bellow, Saul, and Cozzens, James Gould. *AUGIE MARCH NO BOKEN. SAN PEDRO— GO NO SONAN,* trans. Motoji Karita and Masao Takahashi. Tokyo: Kochi Shuppan-sha, 1959.*

E 34
S/S SAN PEDRO, trans. Knud Søgaard. Copenhagen: Gyldendal, 1964.

Appendices / Index

Appendix 1

Movies Made from Cozzens' Works

1.1
Dr. Bull. Fox, 1933. Screenplay from *The Last Adam* by Paul Green. Directed by John Ford.

1.2
By Love Possessed. United Artists, 1961. Screenplay by John Dennis. Directed by John Sturges.

Note: An unidentified short was made from the story, "Foot in It."

Appendix 2

Compiler's Notes

1. In 1927 Cozzens was writing a book on Woodrow Wilson, possibly a ghost-writing assignment. Nothing is known about possible publication. About this time he appears to have accepted several ghosting and editorial assignments for Brandt & Brandt, a literary agency. See Section AA.

2. In March 1928 Cozzens had a job with a New York advertising agency, M. P. Gould & Co., where he worked on the U.S. Bond and Mortgage Corporation account.

3. Cozzens was assigned to the Air Force School of Applied Tactics, Training Aids Division in Washington, Orlando, and New York from September 1942 to fall 1944. He worked on manuals and in 1943 probably contributed material to *TAD*, the newsletter of the Training Aids Division. No run of *TAD* volume I has been located.

4. In 1943 Cozzens worked on revisions of two Air Force manuals: *Tactics and Technique of Air Fighting* (FM 1-15) and *Radio-telephone Procedure* (TM 1-460). His work on FM 1-15 was not used, but his revision of TM 1-460 may have been printed.

5. One signed article by Cozzens appeared in *Air Force* (C 76), but there may have been other anonymous or ghosted contributions.

6. In October 1944 Cozzens was transferred to the Hq. AAF Pentagon staff (Office of Special Projects, Office of Technical Information) and spent the rest of the war ghost-writing reports, speeches, and articles. He probably wrote the message from Gen. H. H. Arnold to the air cadets at West Point in *The Pointer*, XXII (20 October 1944), 1. He also probably wrote the statement by Gen. Clayton Bissell in *Aerosphere 1943* (New York: Aeropshere, 1944), p. XCVII.

7. When this bibliography was in page proof the following entry was discovered, which should follow B 1:

CORYDON | AND OTHER POEMS | BY | LUCIUS M. BEEBE | Boston | B. J. Brimmer Company | 1924.

2-line epigraph for "The King Is Dead," p. 49.

8. The King Features syndication of "The Cockfight" by Cozzens has not been located; it may have been an excerpt from *Cockpit*.

Appendix 3

Books and Pamphlets About Cozzens

Bracher, Frederick. *The Novels of James Gould Cozzens*. New York: Harcourt, Brace, 1959.

Bruccoli, Matthew J., ed. *James Gould Cozzens: New Acquist of True Experience*. Carbondale & Edwardsville: Southern Illinois University Press, 1979.

Hicks, Granville. *James Gould Cozzens*. University of Minnesota Pamphlets on American Writers, no. 58. Minneapolis: University of Minnesota, 1966.

Maxwell, D. E. S. *Cozzens*. Edinburgh & London: Oliver & Boyd, 1964.

Meriwether, James B. *James Gould Cozzens: A Checklist*. Detroit: Bruccoli Clark/Gale, 1972.

Michel, Pierre. *James Gould Cozzens*. New York: Twayne, 1974.

————. *James Gould Cozzens: An Annotated Checklist*. Kent, Ohio: Kent State University Press, 1971.

Mooney, Harry J., Jr. *James Gould Cozzens: Novelist of Intellect*. Pittsburgh: University of Pittsburgh Press, 1963.

Index